Other Kaplan High School Books

Essential Review: High School Biology

Essential Review: High School Chemistry

Essential Review: High School Mathematics II

Essential Review: High School Mathematics III

High School 411

Essential Review

High School MATHEMATICS I

Ira Ewen, M.S.
Principal, James Madison High School (retired)
Brooklyn, NY

Mark Weinfeld, M.A.
MathWorks
New York, NY

Judith Covington, Ph.D.
Louisiana State University
Shreveport, LA

Douglas Smith
Arthur P. Schalick High School
Elmer, NJ

Simon & Schuster

Kaplan Books
Published by Kaplan Educational Centers and Simon & Schuster
1230 Avenue of the Americas
New York, New York 10020

For bulk sales to schools, colleges, and universities, please contact Vice President of Special Sales, Simon & Schuster Special Markets, 1633 Broadway, 8th Floor, New York, NY 10019.

Project Editors: Eileen Mager, Richard Christiano
Contributing Editors: Gregg Driben, Marti Garlett
Cover Design: Cheung Tai
Production Editor: Maude Spekes
Interior Design and Production: James Stirling
Desktop Publishing Manager: Michael Shevlin
Managing Editor: David Chipps
Executive Editor: Del Franz

Special thanks are extended to Robert Marantz, Larissa Shmailo, and Sara Pearl.

Library of Congress Cataloging-in-Publication data is available.

Manufactured in the United States of America
Published Simultaneously in Canada

The practice tests in this book are reprinted by permission of the University of the State of New York/State Education Department.

The testing strategies in chapter 1, "Test Taking," are excerpted from *Learning Power*, by Cynthia Johnson and Drew Johnson (published by Kaplan and Simon & Schuster), and are used by permission. The information on handling stress in chapter 1 is excerpted from "The Kaplan Advantage™ Stress Management System," by Dr. Ed Newman and Bob Verini, copyright © 1996, Kaplan Educational Centers.

October 1999

10 9 8 7 6 5 4 3 2 1

ISBN 0-684-86822-9

CONTENTS

How to Use This Book

This book is designed to supplement your textbook and your class notes. As a general outline to the material you are studying, it contains the most important facts you'll need to remember to do well on your class tests, midterms, and finals. It's a powerful tool, for the student who can use it correctly. Here's how to make your test scores higher:

Study Tips

The first chapter contains some general strategies for doing well on tests. . . strategies that you may not have learned in school. Read through it and remember the valuable advice it contains.

Diagnostic Test

The first practice test is a diagnostic test—by taking it and checking your answers, you will be able to identify your weak points and begin your work of shoring them up. The answer to every question will point you to the chapter in the book where problems like the one tested in the question are further explained. Consult the relevant chapter in your texbook to further solidify your understanding of each concept.

Content Review

The chapters after the diagnostic test are a comprehensive review of the material you are learning in class. Read these in the order that will help you best. For example, if you're preparing for a final exam, you can hit the chapters you identified as weak points in the diagnostic test first, and then read all of the others later. Or, if you're studying for a weekly test, you can concentrate only on the topics that will be tested. Or, if you have some time on your hands, you can start at the beginning and read straight through to the end. There is no wrong way to read it . . . the most important thing is that you get the information you need to do well.

Practice Tests

This book contains five practice tests (the diagnostic test in the beginning of the book, and four others at the end). These are closer in difficulty to a final exam than they are to an ordinary test, but don't panic: You're the only one who will see your scores, and you have the benefit of filling the gaps in your knowledge before you're tested for real in school. If you can do well on these tests, you're well on the road to mastering this subject!

Part I

Study Tips

Chapter 1

Studying for Success in Mathematics

You are going to do well on your mathematics tests.

You are going do well because you will believe in yourself, because you will know the mathematics, and because you will have practiced enough of the problems so that your next test will look familiar and nonfrightening.

Think about some long-range goals, beyond the mere passing of tests, that are within your reach with some additional effort:

- You can learn mathematics well enough to carry over the summer break and assist you in doing even better in your next course.

- You can learn mathematics well enough to be able to apply the *concepts* and *skills* in new contexts such as science, economics, or business.

- You can learn mathematics well enough to be able to apply what you have learned in unfamiliar settings and to problem situations in which you are not certain how to begin or where you are going. (Such situations, formally called *ill-defined problem situations*, occur continually in life. They occur at home, on the job, in school, and in your interaction with friends.)

- You can learn mathematics well enough so that you will think of yourself as mathematically able.

Here are some of the things you can do so that the effort you put into your tests will reward you far beyond the day you get your passing grade.

Reflect on Your Work

After each problem you do, take a few seconds to think about the problem. What mathematical concepts were involved? Which part of the problem gave you difficulty? What question about the ideas behind the problem could you ask a teacher about?

Reflection is thinking about what you have done, what you have heard, what has happened to you so that you can learn from the experience. Some people reflect on each day in their lives because they want to avoid repeating avoidable mistakes. Yet few students—or teachers—have reflected on the major concepts of their subject. What are the major concepts of mathematics? Which of these concepts applies to the current problem (or the current lesson, or the current topic)?

For your guidance, here are eleven concepts central to mathematics:

1. Sameness and equivalence

2. Evidence and certainty

3. Measure and measurement

4. Symbols and meaning

5. Characteristics and representation of data

6. Symmetry

7. Relations and functions

8. Invariance

9. Operations

10. Inference

11. Mathematical systems and models

This is not a complete list, but you might want to reflect on where other topics fit on this partial list. *Probability*? Probability is a *measure* (concept 3) of events; the study of probability is related closely to the study of length, area, and volume. *Statistics*? The mean, median, mode, range, and dozens of other measures (concept 3) are characteristics of *data* (concept 5). *Graphs and charts* are also representations of data. *Slope* is a *measure* (concept 3) of a line and an *invariant* (concept 8) in a set of parallel lines.

The act of thinking about questions such as this is a powerful mode of study. It makes connections, fixes ideas in your long-term memory (the memory that lingers after tomorrow), and puts you in charge of what you are trying to learn.

Keep a Journal

A simple route to productive reflection is to keep a brief daily mathematics journal. Identify the major mathematical concepts of each day's lesson and apply those concepts to another mathematical topic or real-life situation. If you can discipline yourself to keep such a journal for two weeks, compare your grades on the material covered during those weeks to your usual grades. You will be pleasantly amazed.

Practice New Ideas by Making Up Problems and Solving Them

A rich technique for solving a verbal problem is to copy down the data and *omit the question*. Explore several things you might be able to deduce from the data given. Write one or two questions based on the data which you could answer. Often you will figure out for yourself what the question in the problem actually was!

In the days before each test, try to make up five to ten problems that would worry you if you found them on the actual test. If you cannot solve them yourself, reflect on why you had difficulty with it. Was it unfamiliarity with the topic, with a skill related to the topic, with the underlying mathematical concept, or with the thinking skills used in analyzing the problem?

Some of the most successful students in high school and college try to predict the questions that will appear on examinations and to answer those questions. They reflect on the way the writer of the test might be thinking. Whether or not they predict the questions correctly, they are studying for the examination in an effective way. Why not try it yourself?

Thinking Skills and Problem Solving Strategies

Several strategies exist that are particularly helpful in mathematics when dealing with unfamiliar problem situations. Here are some of the most frequently applicable strategies.

Working backwards. Whenever there are several possible ways to begin and a limited objective, working backward is helpful. A good example is the proof that $\sqrt{2}$ is irrational. Because you cannot see how to begin a direct proof, you begin backward, saying, "Suppose $\sqrt{2}$ is rational." You then follow an argument that leads you to a contradiction of the theorem that every rational number can be reduced to lowest terms as a quotient of integers. Even when you know this proof very well, you would be hard put to make it into a direct proof. There are countless situations in mathematics and in life when working backward is advisable.

Finding a pattern. In mathematics, some challenging problems are easily solved if a pattern is uncovered. A teacher challenges you to count accurately the number of diagonals in a (convex) 12-sided polygon (which is known to mathematicians as a convex dodecagon). Drawing a figure and attempting to draw in all the diagonals is difficult. So try looking at simpler polygons, making a chart listing the number of sides in each polygon in the first column and the number of diagonals in the second column. With a little effort you get down to 7-sided polygons (heptagons) and your table looks like this:

number of sides	number of diagonals
3	0
4	2
5	5
6	9
7	14

You don't know *why* this pattern is developing, but you notice that the righthand column increases first by 2, then by 3, then by 4, and then by 5. Each time you increase the number of sides by 1, the number of diagonals increases by a whole number one greater than the one for the prior increase. You conjecture that the table will continue to follow that pattern:

number of sides	number of diagonals
8	20
9	27
10	35
11	44
12	54

You have made an educated guess based on limited evidence. Giving your teacher your conjecture and your evidence has a far better chance of getting you recognition than presenting a cluttered diagram with missing or miscounted diagonals.

In time you may even become skillful at explaining *why the pattern develops*. If that happens, you will be functioning much like a professional mathematician.

Adopting a different point of view. How could a strategy like this apply to mathematics? Suppose you are having difficulty understanding why the textbook has defined $x^0 = 1$, for $x \neq 0$. Instead of merely stewing about it, you decide to change your point of view and look for a pattern that might help you to understand the definition. You note that in order to get from x^4 to x^3, you divide by x. To get from x^3 to x^2, you divide by x. To get from x^2 to x^1, you divide by x, getting $x^1 = x$. You conjecture that in order to get from x^1 to x^0, you might expect to have to divide by x. Since $x \div x = 1$ (for $x \neq 0$), you can now accept the definition $x^0 = 1$ more easily.

Solving a Simpler Analogous Problem. People often do not immediately see the easiest way to do something. Solving a simpler analogous problem can lead you to a simple or complicated answer in easy steps that you will be able to construct and understand.

Let us say you are asked to determine the change in the product xy from the case when $x = y$ to the case when x is increased by 7 and y is decreased by 7. You decide to use simpler (smaller) numbers and make a chart when 1 is the increase/decrease instead of 7. You write:

Original value of x	Original value of xy	Final value of xy
1	$1 \cdot 1 = 1$	$2 \cdot 0 = 0$
2	$2 \cdot 2 = 4$	$3 \cdot 1 = 3$
3	$3 \cdot 3 = 9$	$4 \cdot 2 = 8$
4	$4 \cdot 4 = 16$	$5 \cdot 3 = 15$
5	$5 \cdot 5 = 25$	$6 \cdot 4 = 24$

In each of these five cases, the product has decreased by 1. Based on the observed pattern (strategy 2), you conjecture that when the increase/decrease is 1, the product always decreases by 1.

You now make a chart for the increase/decrease 2.

Original value of x	Original value of xy	Final value of xy
1	$1 \cdot 1 = 1$	$3 \cdot (-1) = -3$
2	$2 \cdot 2 = 4$	$4 \cdot 0 = 0$
3	$3 \cdot 3 = 9$	$5 \cdot 1 = 5$
4	$4 \cdot 4 = 16$	$6 \cdot 2 = 12$
5	$5 \cdot 5 = 25$	$7 \cdot 3 = 21$

In each of these five cases, the product has decreased by 4. Based on the observed pattern (strategy 2), you conjecture that when the increase/decrease is 2, the product always decreases by 4.

You now make charts for the increase/decrease 3, for 4, and for 5. You make another chart showing your results:

Increase/Decrease	Change in Product
1	Decreases by 1
2	Decreases by 4
3	Decreases by 9
4	Decreases by 16
5	Decreases by 25

Based on the observed pattern you conjecture that for any increase/decrease, the product will always decrease by its *square*. For the case when the increase/decrease is 7, you expect the product to decrease by 49.

Considering extreme cases. Speakers often use extreme cases to provide a useful analogy. When you use this strategy, you must be aware that the extreme cases may give insight but they may lead to incorrect conjectures. So long as you *reflect* on what you do, you can benefit from the insights and reject the incorrect conjectures.

For example, if someone tells you that a formula works for all numbers, test the formula for 0 and for 1 (the simplest cases) and for some outlandish number such as 1739. If the formula checks out in those three cases, although you have not proved it *always* works, it has a lot of believability.

Remember to *examine* the extremes, but never *depend unthinkingly* on them.

Using visual representation. Sometimes a picture helps you to solve a very tricky problem.

A jogger leaves home at 6 A.M. and jogs at an irregular pace along a narrow path arriving at his destination at 7 A.M. that morning. He spends 23 hours at his destination. The next day he reverses his path and jogs at an irregular pace back home leaving for home at 6 A.M. and arriving at 7 A.M. Under what conditions must there have been a place in the road which he reached at *exactly the same time* both days?

Believe it or not, there always must be such a place somewhere along his route. If it's not obvious, draw a pair of graphs on the same axes, labeling the x-axis with time and the y-axis with distance from his home. Somewhere, the two curves in each graph cross each other. At the time and place represented in each graph—the intersection—the jogger was in exactly the same place at exactly the same time on the two days.

Making intelligent guesses. On a short-answer test, it is often advisable to take a shortcut to an answer by smart guessing and testing. Consider the following problem: Find three consecutive integers with product 5,814.

Setting up algebraic equations is time-consuming and difficult. You think: If the three numbers were the same, they would be the cube root of 5,814. Take out your handy calculator and compute $\sqrt[3]{5,814}$. The calculator gives you 17.98146. You guess that 18 is the middle number, and the three numbers are 17, 18, and 19. You again use your calculator to check. Sure enough, $17 \cdot 18 \cdot 19 = 5,814$.

Guessing has gotten a bad reputation because of two major difficulties: (1) teachers want students to do a problem a certain way and discourage shortcuts; (2) students tend to guess rather randomly, saying almost anything. When you make an intelligent guess, you must have a reason for your guess—it must be based on knowledge and sound intuition.

Using This Book

You will derive maximum benefit from this book by playing with the problems throughout. Reflect on them, change them, and find the central concepts they illustrate. See if you can solve each problem in more than one way, perhaps by using a different thinking strategy. When you find more than one way to do a problem, think about when you would use each approach.

Keep a "tough" file of problems that you found extremely difficult. Talk to friends and teachers about the problem and include repeated attacks on the problems in your tough file in your study plan. Nothing builds confidence as much as gaining a thorough understanding of a problem that initially stumped you.

The suggestions made in this section will help you to do well on your mathematics tests. And you might just find that the next math course you take will be easier and more fun than any you've taken before.

Part II

Diagnostic Test

Practice Test 1: Diagnostic Test

Part I

Answer 30 questions from this part. Each correct answer will receive 2 credits. No partial credit will be allowed. Write your answers in the spaces provided on the separate answer sheet. Where applicable, answers may be left in terms of π or in radical form. [60]

1 Solve for x: $5(2x - 4) = 10$

2 Two angles of a triangle have measures of 30 and 55. Find the measure of the third angle.

3 Solve for x: $\dfrac{2x}{3} = \dfrac{8}{6}$

4 Solve for x: $0.15x = 5.25$

5 Alice has 6 dresses, 2 coats, and 3 hats. How many different outfits can she wear consisting of a dress, a coat, and a hat?

6 Let p represent "It is winter" and let q represent "I go swimming." Using p and q, write in symbolic form: "If I do *not* go swimming, then it is winter."

7 Solve for x: $5x - 21 = 8x - 30$

8 If 80% of a number is 24, what is the number?

9 In the accompanying diagram of circle O, arc ACB has a measure of 280. What is the measure of central angle x?

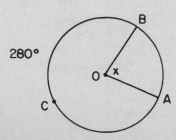

10 In the accompanying diagram, parallel lines $\overleftrightarrow{AB}$ and $\overleftrightarrow{CD}$ are intersected by transversal $\overleftrightarrow{EF}$ at points G and H, respectively. If the measure of angle EGB is $3x$ and the measure of angle CHF is 84, find the value of x.

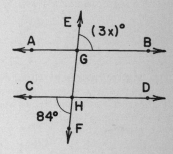

11 If a number is picked at random from the set $\{1,2,3,4\}$, what is the probability that the number is a solution for $2x + 5 > 7$?

12 The perimeter of a square is $4x - 8$. Express the length of one side of the square in terms of x.

13 The sides of a triangle are 12, 15, and 20. If the shortest side of a similar triangle is 3, find the length of the longest side of that triangle.

14 Simplify by combining like terms:

$$(5a + 3b) + 2(a - 3b)$$

15 If the circumference of a circle is 28π, what is the radius of that circle?

16 Factor: $x^2 - 16x + 48$

17 Solve for x in terms of a, b, and c:

$$bx + c = a$$

18 Express the sum of $\frac{x}{3}$ and $\frac{x}{5}$ as a single fraction in lowest terms.

19 Express the product $(2x - 3)(x + 5)$ as a trinomial.

20 Solve the following system of equations for x:

$$3x + y = 11$$
$$2x - y = -1$$

21 Find the value of the expression $2xy^3$ if $x = 3$ and $y = -2$.

Directions (22–35): For *each* question chosen, write on the separate answer sheet the *numeral* preceding the word or expression that best completes the statement or answers the question.

22 The quotient $\frac{16x^3y^5}{4xy^2}$ is equivalent to

(1) $4x^2y^3$ (3) $12x^2y^3$

(2) $4xy^7$ (4) $12x^3y^3$

23 In a class there are 11 boys and 14 girls. What is the ratio of the number of girls in the class to the number of pupils in the class?

(1) $\frac{11}{14}$ (3) $\frac{14}{25}$

(2) $\frac{14}{11}$ (4) $\frac{25}{14}$

24 For which group of data does the mean equal the mode?

(1) 4,4,5,6   (3) 4,5,5,6

(2) 4,5,6,6   (4) 4,5,5,8

25 If $p \lor q$ is false, then
(1) both p and q are true
(2) p is false and q is true
(3) p is true and q is false
(4) both p and q are false

26 If $V = \ell wh$, what is the value of V when $\ell = 2$, $w = 3$, and $h = 4x$?
(1) $9x$ (3) $5 + 4x$
(2) $24x$ (4) $6 + 4x$

27 If point $(b,4)$ is in the solution set of $3x + y = 13$, then the value of b must be
(1) 1   (3) 3
(2) 2   (4) 4

28 The value of $\frac{5!}{3!}$ is

(1) 20   (3) 5
(2) 2   (4) 4

29 The inverse of $p \rightarrow \sim q$ is
(1) $q \rightarrow \sim p$ (3) $\sim p \rightarrow \sim q$
(2) $q \rightarrow p$ (4) $\sim p \rightarrow q$

30 What is the slope of the line whose equation is $y = -3x + 6$?

(1) $-\frac{1}{2}$ (3) -3

(2) 2   (4) 6

31 Which represents a rational number?

(1) π (3) $\sqrt{15}$

(2) $\sqrt{16}$ (4) $\sqrt{\frac{100}{5}}$

32 Which graph represents the solution of the inequality $2x + 3 > 9$?

(1)

(2)

(3)

(4)

33 The solution set of $x^2 - 64 = 0$ is
  (1) $\{8,-8\}$ (3) $\{8\}$
  (2) $\{-8\}$ (4) $\{16,-4\}$

34 Which is equivalent to $4\sqrt{3}$?
  (1) 144   (3) $\sqrt{19}$
  (2) $\sqrt{48}$ (4) $\sqrt{16}$

35 Which expression is undefined if $x = 6$?
  (1) x^0 (3) $\dfrac{1}{x+6}$

  (2) $x - 6$ (4) $\dfrac{1}{x-6}$

Answers to the following questions are to be written on paper provided by the school.

Part II

Answer four questions from this part. Show all work unless otherwise directed.   [40]

36 Solve graphically and check:

$$2x + y = 5$$
$$x - 2y = 10 \qquad \text{[8,2]}$$

37 One integer is 4 more than three times another integer. The sum of the two integers is less than 21. Find the *largest* possible values for both integers. [*Only an algebraic solution will be accepted.*]   [5,5]

38 In the accompanying diagram, $\overline{AB}$ is a diameter of circle O, the measure of $\angle BAC$ is 40, and the measure of $\overset{\frown}{AD}$ is 70.

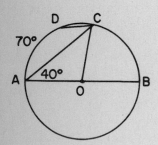

a Find the measure of minor arc BC.   [2]
b Find m$\angle BOC$.   [2]
c Find m$\angle ACD$.   [2]
d Find the measure of minor arc CD.   [2]
e Find m$\angle AOC$.   [2]

39 The length of the hypotenuse of a right triangle is 13. The length of the shorter leg is 7 less than the length of the longer leg. Find the length of the *shorter* leg. [*Only an algebraic solution will be accepted.*]   [5,5]

40 In △ABC, $\angle B$ is congruent to $\angle C$. The measure of $\angle B$ is 20 more than twice the measure of $\angle A$. Find the measure of *each* angle in △ABC. [*Only an algebraic solution will be accepted.*]   [6,4]

41 The table below represents the ages of high school principals in a large city.

Interval	Frequency
68–75	5
60–67	10
52–59	25
44–51	15
36–43	25
28–35	20

a Which interval contains the median?   [2]
b If a principal is chosen at random, what is the probability that the age of the principal is in the interval 44–51?   [2]
c What is the probability that the age of a principal is less than 44?   [2]
d What is the probability that a principal is younger than 28?   [2]
e What percent of the principals' ages are in the interval 52–59?   [2]

☞ GO RIGHT ON TO THE NEXT PAGE.

42 *On your answer paper*, copy and complete the truth table for the statement
$(\sim p \lor q) \longrightarrow [q \land (p \rightarrow \sim q)]$.   [10]

p	q	$\sim p$	$\sim p \lor q$	$\sim q$	$p \rightarrow \sim q$	$q \land (p \rightarrow \sim q)$	$(\sim p \lor q) \longrightarrow [q \land (p \rightarrow \sim q)]$
T	T						
T	F						
F	T						
F	F						

Practice Test 1: Diagnostic Test

Answers

1. $x = 3$

$5(2x - 4) = 10$	Distribute.
$10x - 20 = 10$	Add 20 to both sides.
$10x - 20 + 20 = 10 + 20$	
$10x = 30$	Divide by 10.
$x = 3$	

   For a review of solving equations, see chapter 3, "Algebra."

2. $95°$

   The sum of the measures of the angles of a triangle is $180°$. Since $30 + 55 = 85$ the remaining angle must be 95.
   See chapter 4, "Geometry," for more information about triangles.

3. $x = 2$

$\frac{2x}{3} = \frac{8}{6}$	Cross multiply.
$12x = 24$	Divide by 12.
$x = 2$	

   If you'd like more practice solving equations, check out chapter 3, "Algebra."

4. $x = 35$

$0.15x = 5.25$	Divide by .15.
$x = 35$	

   You can review these steps in chapter 3, "Algebra."

5. 36 different outfits.

   There are three choices and we use the multiplication principle and multiply. There are six choices for a dress, 2 for a coat, and 3 for a hat. So there are $6 \times 2 \times 3 = 36$ different outfits.
   This counting principle is covered in chapter 6, "Probability."

6. $\sim q \rightarrow p$

   If you do not swim, that is not q represented by $\sim q$. Then is equivalent to $\rightarrow$. And p represents winter.
   Review Logic in chapter 2, "Logic."

7. $x = 3$

$5x - 21 = 8x - 30$	Subtract $5x$ from both sides.
$5x - 21 - 5x = 8x - 30 - 5x$	
$-21 = 3x - 30$	Add 30 to both sides.
$-21 + 30 = 3x - 30 + 30$	
$9 = 3x$	Divide by 3.
$3 = x$	

   For a review of solving equations, see chapter 3, "Algebra."

8. The number is 30.

   80 percent is $\frac{80}{100}$. We want 24 out of an unknown number. So $\frac{24}{x}$. Set these as equal.

$\frac{80}{100} = \frac{24}{x}$	Cross multiply.
$80x = 2,400$	Divide by 80.

$x = 30$

If you'd like more practice solving equations, check out chapter 3, "Algebra."

9. 80°

The measure of the central angle is the same as the measure of the arc it intercepts. Since $\text{m}\overset{\frown}{ACB} = 280$, then $\text{m}\overset{\frown}{AB} = 360 - 280 = 80$. So $x = 80$.

10. $x = 28$

$\angle EGB$ and $\angle CHF$ are alternate exterior angles and since lines $\overleftrightarrow{AB}$ and $\overleftrightarrow{CD}$ are parallel, the angles have the same measure.

$3x = 84$ Divide by 3.

$x = 28$

You can review the properties of parallel lines in chapter 4, "Geometry."

11. $\frac{3}{4}$

Solve $2x + 5 > 7$.   Subtract 5 from both sides.

$2x + 5 - 5 > 7 - 5$

$2x > 2$ Divide by 2.

$x > 1$

There are 3 elements from the set satisfying the inequality (2, 3, 4) and there are 4 total elements in the set. The probability is thus $\frac{3}{4}$.

Probability is covered in chapter 6, "Probability."

12. $x - 2$

The perimeter of a square is 4 times the length of a side. Since $4x - 8 = 4(x - 2)$ the length of the side is $x - 2$.

You can review solving equations in chapter 3, "Algebra," and perimeter in chapter 4, "Geometry."

13. 5

In similar triangles, corresponding sides have the same ratio. Thus,

$\frac{3}{12} = \frac{\ell}{20}$ Cross multiply.

$60 = 12\ell$ Divide by 12.

$5 = \ell$

Triangles are covered in chapter 4, "Geometry."

14. $7a - 3b$

$(5a + 3b) + 2(a - 3b)$ Distribute.

$5a + 3b + 2a - 6b$ Combine like terms.

$7a - 3b$

For more information on solving equations like this, see chapter 3, "Algebra."

15. 14

Since the circumference is 2 times π times the radius,

$28\pi = 2\pi r$ Divide by 2π.

$14 = r$

You can review circumference in chapter 4, "Geometry."

16. $(x - 12)(x - 4)$

    You need to find factors of 48 that add up to 16. These are 12 and 4.
    For more information on factoring trinomials, see chapter 3, "Algebra."

17. $\dfrac{a - c}{b}$

    $bx + c = a$ Subtract c from both sides.
    $bx + c - c = a - c$
    $bx = a - c$ Divide by b.
    $x = \dfrac{a - c}{b}$
    Refer to chapter 3, "Algebra," to review "solving in terms of."

18. $\dfrac{8x}{15}$

    Rewrite with a common denominator of 15.
    $\dfrac{x}{3} + \dfrac{x}{5} = \dfrac{5x}{15} + \dfrac{3x}{15} = \dfrac{8x}{15}$

    For more on common denominators, see chapter 3, "Algebra."

19. $2x^2 + 7x - 15$

    Distribute.
    $2x(x + 5) - 3(x + 5)$
    $2x^2 + 10x - 3x - 15$
    $2x^2 + 7x - 15$
    For a review of distributing factors, refer to chapter 3, "Algebra."

20. $x = 2$

    Add equations together to eliminate y.
    $3x + y = 11$
    $\underline{2x - y = -1}$
    $5x \quad\;\; = 10$ Divide by 5.
    $x = 2$
    For further review of solving a system of equations, see chapter 5, "Analytic Geometry."

21. -48

    Substitute 3 for x and -2 for y
    $2(3)(-2)^3 = 2(3)(-8) = -\mathbf{48}$
    You can review algebraic substitution in chapter 3, "Algebra."

22. (1) $4x^2y^3$

    Reduce by canceling common factors.
    $4x^2y^3$
    $\dfrac{16x^3y^5}{4xy} = 4x^2y^3$
    See chapter 3, "Algebra," for more on canceling common factors.

23. (3) $\dfrac{14}{25}$

    There are 14 girls in the class and 25 total pupils in the class. $(11 + 14 = 25)$
    Ratios are covered in chapter 6, "Probability."

24. (3) 4, 5, 5, 6

    The mode is 5 because it occurs most often. The mean is also 5 since
    $\dfrac{4 + 5 + 5 + 6}{4} = 5$
    Mean and mode are covered in chapter 7, "Statistics."

25. (4) both p and q are false.

    The symbol $\vee$ represents *or*.
    Is your logic rusty? Check out chapter 2, "Logic," for a refresher course.

26. (2) $24x$

    Substitute
    $V = lwh = (2)(3)(4x) = 24x$

    Substitution is covered in chapter 3, "Algebra."

27. (3) 3

    Substitute 4 for y and solve for x.

    $3x + 4 = 13$ 	Subtract 4 from both sides.

    $3x + 4 - 4 = 13 - 4$

    $3x = 9$ 	Divide by 3.

    $x = 3$

    For more on the method of solving a system of equations, see chapter 5, "Analytic Geometry.

28. (1) 20

    Simplify by rewriting and canceling common factors. $\dfrac{5!}{3!} = \dfrac{5 \cdot 4 \cdot \cancel{3} \cdot \cancel{2} \cdot \cancel{1}}{\cancel{3} \cdot \cancel{2} \cdot \cancel{1}} = 20$

    Permutations, or "factorials," are covered in chapter 6, "Probability."

29. (4) $\sim p \rightarrow \sim q$

    Negate each statement. The negation of p is $\sim p$. The negation of $\sim q$ is q.
    Review Logic in chapter 2, "Logic."

30. (3) -3

    If the equation is solved for y, the coefficient of x is the slope.
    To review slope, see chapter 5, "Analytic Geometry."

31. (2) $\sqrt{16}$

    Because 16 is a perfect square, $\sqrt{16} = 4$.

    For more on radicals, see chapter 3, "Algebra."

32. (3)

    $2x + 3 > 9$ 	Subtract 3 from both sides.

    $2x + 3 - 3 > 9 - 3$

    $2x > 6$ 	Divide by 2.

    $x > 3$

    We want numbers greater than 3 but not including 3.

    You can review inequalities in chapter 5, "Analytic Geometry."

33. (1)

    $x^2 - 64 = 0$ 	Add 64 to both sides.

    $x^2 = 64$ 	Take square root of both sides.

    $x = \pm\sqrt{64}$ 	Remember $+$ and $-$.

    $x = \pm 8$ 	There are two numbers which squared equal 64. They are 8 and -8.

    For more information on solving equations like this, see chapter 3, "Algebra."

34 (2)

$$\sqrt{48} = \sqrt{16} \cdot \sqrt{3} = 4\sqrt{3}$$

You can review radicals in chapter 3, "Algebra."

35. (4)

Because 6 makes the denominator equal zero. For more on number properties, see chapter 3, "Algebra."

36. Graph each equation and see where the graphs intersect.

To graph $2x + y = 5$, let $x = 0$, find y, then let $y = 0$, find x.

If $x = 0$, $y = 5$. If $y = 0$, $x = \frac{5}{2}$.

To graph $x - 2y = 10$, do the same.

If $x = 0$, $y = -5$. If $y = 0$, $x = 10$.

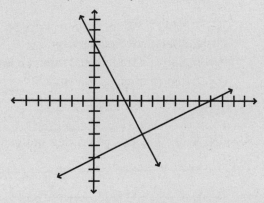

Graphing equations is covered in chapter 5, "Analytic Geometry."

The intersection is $(4, -3)$

Check: $2(4) - 3 = 5$; $8 - 3 = 5$. Checks.

Check: $4 - 2(-3) = 10$; $4 + 6 = 10$. Checks.

37. Let $x =$ first integer.

Then $3x + 4 =$ next integer.

$x + 3x + 4 < 21$

$4x + 4 < 21$ Subtract 4 from both sides.

$4x + 4 - 4 < 21 - 4$

$4x < 17$ Divide by 4.

$x < 4\frac{1}{4}$

The integers are 4 and $3(4) + 4 = 16$.

See chapter 3, "Algebra," for a review of solving equations.

38. a.   80

The inscribed angle has a measure of 40° and the intercepted arc is double that.

b.   80

$\angle BOC$ is a central angle and has the measure of the arc it intercepts.

c.   35

$\angle ACD$ is an inscribed angle and has measure half of its intercepted arc.

d.   30

$m\overset{\frown}{AB} = 180$ since AB is a diameter. Then

$m\overset{\frown}{AD} + m\overset{\frown}{CD} + m\overset{\frown}{BC} = 180$

$70 + m\overset{\frown}{CD} + 80 = 180$

$m\overset{\frown}{CD} = 30$

e.   100

$\angle AOC$ is a central angle intercepting arc$\overset{\frown}{AC}$. $m\overset{\frown}{AC} = 100$. So that is the measure of the angle.

Circles and their angles are covered in chapter 4, "Geometry."

39. 5

Let ℓ = length of long leg. Then $\ell - 7$ = length of short leg.

Using the Pythagorean Theorem,

$13^2 = \ell^2 + (\ell - 7)^2$

$169 = \ell^2 + \ell^2 - 14\ell + 49$ Subtract 169 from both sides.

$0 = 2\ell^2 - 14\ell - 120$ Divide by 2.

$0 = \ell^2 - 7\ell - 60$

$0 = (\ell - 12)(\ell + 5)$ Set each factor equal to 0.

$\ell - 12 = 0 \quad \ell + 5 = 0$

$\ell = 12 \qquad \ell = -5$ not possible

$\ell - 7 = 5$

For a review of the Pythagorean Theorem, see chapter 4, "Geometry."

40. $m\angle A = 28°, m\angle B = 76°, m\angle C = 76°$

Let $x = m\angle A$, then

$2x + 20 = m\angle B = m\angle C$

The sum of the angles is 180

$x + 2x + 20 + 2x + 20 = 180$

$5x + 40 = 180$ Subtract 40.

$5x = 140$ Divide by 5.

$x = 28$

$m\angle A = 28, m\angle B = m\angle C = 76$

Triangles are covered in chapter 4, "Geometry."

41. a.   44–51

There are 100 observations so the median is between the 50th and 51st observation. These are both in the interval 44–51.

b. $\dfrac{15}{100}$

There are 15 observations in this interval out of a total of 100 observations.

c. $\dfrac{45}{100}$

There are 45 observations less than 44.

d.   0

There are no principals younger than 28.

e.   25 percent

$\dfrac{25}{100} = 25$ percent

Probability is covered in chapter 6, "Probability." Median and intervals are covered in chapter 7, "Statistics."

42. See below.

See chapter 2, "Logic," for a review of this topic.

p	q	$\sim p$	$\sim p \vee q$	$\sim q$	$p \rightarrow \sim q$	$q \wedge (p \rightarrow \sim q)$	$(\sim p \vee q) \leftrightarrow [q \wedge (p \rightarrow \sim q)]$
T	T	F	T	F	F	F	F
T	F	F	F	T	T	F	T
F	T	T	T	F	T	T	T
F	F	T	T	T	T	F	F

Part III

Math I Review

Chapter 2

Logic

A. Closed and open sentences

Statements in logic are classified in two main categories, closed and open. A closed statement is one that can definitively be said to be either true or false. An open statement is one whose truth value cannot be determined.

For any open statement, there may be values that would make it true. These values are called the solution set of the statement.

Examples:

Are these statements closed or open? If they are closed, are they true or false?

The sum of two negative numbers is a negative number.

> This is a closed statement. It is also true.

z is divisible by 5.

> This is an open statement. There are certain solutions that will make the sentence true, for example, 5, 10, and −20, but since we do not know what the value of z is, the statement is open. The solution set would be the set of all numbers divisible by 5, which can be written $\{\ldots-5, 0, 5, 10 \ldots\}$

1 is a prime number.

> This is a closed statement. By definition, 1 is not a prime number, so the statement is false.

B.   The algebra of logic

Just as arithmetic has symbols for addition, division, equality, etcetera, logic has its symbols as well. First, any statement can be represented by a letter. For example, the statement "It is sunny today" might be called statement p. The statement, "I am going to the movies," could be called statement q. In algebra, we usually use x and y to stand for numbers. In logic, we usually use p and q to stand for statements.

There are certain words that can be used to connect statements together to form compound statements. These words also have symbols which represent them. They are:

$\lor$—or.   An "or" statement is called a *disjunction*.

$\land$—and.   An "and" statement is called a *conjunction*.

$\rightarrow$—if-then.   The "if-then" statement is called a *conditional*.

$\Leftrightarrow$—if and only if.   The "if and only if" statement is called a *biconditional*.

Any statement p can be "negated," or reversed. The symbol for negation is a tilde, $\sim$, and the statement $\sim p$ is read as "not p."

Examples:

If the statement p is "x is even," and statement q is "x is prime," then what do these statements say?

$\sim p$ The tilde stands for the negation of statement p, so instead of reading that "x is even" we read "x is not even." It is always preferable to use the "not" in your statement, since changing the entire wording of the statement may distort the meaning of the statement.

$p \lor q$ The symbol $\lor$ represents the word *or*, so the statement says "x is even or x is prime."

$q \rightarrow \sim p$ The symbol $\rightarrow$ represents the words *if-then*, so the statement says "If x is prime, then x is not even."

$p \Leftrightarrow q$ The symbol $\Leftrightarrow$ represents the words *if and only if*, so the statement says "x is even if and only if x is prime."

$\sim q \land p$ The symbol $\land$ represents the word *and*, so the statement says "x is not prime and x is even."

Related conditionals

a. The *converse* of a conditional statement $p \rightarrow q$ is the statement $q \rightarrow p$, formed by interchanging the hypothesis and the conclusion.

b. The *inverse of* $p \rightarrow q$ is the statement $(\sim p) \rightarrow (\sim q)$, formed by negating both the hypothesis and the conclusion.

c. The *contrapositive* of $p \rightarrow q$ is the statement $(\sim q) \rightarrow (\sim p)$, formed by negating and interchanging the roles of the hypothesis and the conclusion.

We can summarize these definitions as follows:

A conditional	If p, then q	$p \rightarrow q$
Its converse	If q, then p	$q \rightarrow p$
Its inverse	If not p, then not q	$(\sim p) \rightarrow (\sim q)$
Its contrapositive	If not q, then not p	$(\sim q) \rightarrow (\sim p)$

C. Truth tables

Compound statements can be represented in a table format. For any two statements p and q, there are four possibilities for the combination of their truth values. They are:

p and q are true

p is true and q is false

p is false and q is true

p and q are false

We can sum up these possibilities in the following chart, which is the first part of any truth table:

p	q
T	T
T	F
F	T
F	F

Consider the disjunction *or* with the following example. Let p = "I have a dime," and q = "I have a quarter." When is the statement "I have a dime or I have a quarter" ($p \lor q$) true overall? It is true when either part of the statement is true, and it is false only when both the parts are false. This can be summed up in the following truth table:

p	q	$p \lor q$
T	T	T
T	F	T
F	T	T
F	F	F

Now consider the conjunction *and*. Using the same two statements p and q, when is the statement "I have a dime and I have a quarter" a true one? The overall statement is true only when both p and q are true, and false for all other cases. This can be summed up in the following truth table:

p	q	$p \land q$
T	T	T
T	F	F
F	T	F
F	F	F

The conditional statement is a tougher one to understand. The statement "If I have a dime, then I have a quarter" is obviously true if I have both a dime and quarter. It is also obviously false if I have a dime but do not have a quarter. But, what is the value of the statement if I don't have a dime to begin with but I do have the quarter? Or what if I have neither a dime nor a quarter? You may think that there can be no definitive answer in these cases, but the rules of logic are that if the premise (the first part or "if" part) is false, the entire statement a true statement. Therefore, the truth table for the conditional is as follows:

p	q	$p \rightarrow q$
T	T	T
T	F	F
F	T	T
F	F	T

The biconditional "if and only if" is really a conditional "if-then" statement applied in both directions. The biconditional $p \Leftrightarrow q$ is the conjunction of the conditionals and $q \rightarrow p$. Thus, $p \rightarrow q$ means $(p \rightarrow q) \wedge (q \rightarrow p)$. Consider the values of $p \rightarrow q$ AND $q \rightarrow p$ for the overall value of $p \Leftrightarrow q$. This means that if p and q are true statements, then the overall value of $p \Leftrightarrow q$ is true. If both statements are false, then the overall truth value of the statement is also true! (by definition of the conditional above). In the other two cases, one of the two directions is a true premise and a false conclusion, which makes the overall statement a false one. The truth table for the biconditional is as follows:

p	q	$p \Leftrightarrow q$
T	T	T
T	F	F
F	T	F
F	F	T

Finally, a truth table where all the values turn out to be true is called a *tautology*. You will see some tautologies in the examples and the exercises.

Examples:

Construct a truth table for $p \rightarrow (q \wedge p)$.

As in algebra, we will follow the order of operations and first make a column for $(q \wedge p)$. Then we will combine this column with the p column for the final column.

p	q	$q \wedge p$	$p \to (q \wedge p)$
T	T	T	T
T	F	F	F
F	T	F	T
F	F	F	T

Construct a truth table for $(p \wedge \sim q) \vee q$.

We need a column for $\sim q$, for $(p \wedge \sim q)$, and then the entire compound statement.

p	q	$\sim q$	$p \wedge \sim q$	$(p \wedge \sim q) \vee q$
T	T	F	F	T
T	F	T	T	T
F	T	F	F	T
F	F	T	F	F

Construct a truth table for $[(p \to q) \wedge p] \to q$

p	q	$p \to q$	$[(p \to q) \wedge p]$	$[(p \to q) \wedge p] \to q$
T	T	T	T	T
T	F	F	F	T
F	T	T	F	T
F	F	T	F	T

This truth table is a tautology.

Questions

Classify these statements as closed or open. If closed, state if they are true or false.

1. 6 is an even number.

2. It will rain here tomorrow.

3. Albany is the capital of New York State.

4. The product of x and y is a positive number.

5. There is no such thing as an even prime number.

6. Tomorrow is Tuesday.

7. $x + 1 = 5$

What is the solution set for the following open statements?

8. $x + 3 > 8$.

9. x is an odd and positive number.

10. B was the first president of the United States.

11. y is a positive factor of 28.

Let p be the statement "y is even," q be the statement "y is odd," and r be the statement "$y = 7$."

What do the following statements say?

12. $p \vee q$

13. $q \rightarrow r$

14. $p \vee q \vee r$

15. $p \wedge \sim p$

16. $r \Leftrightarrow q$

17. $(p \vee q) \rightarrow r$

18. $\sim p \rightarrow p$

19. $\sim q \Leftrightarrow \sim r$

20. $\sim r \wedge (p \rightarrow q)$

21. $(\sim q \vee \sim r) \wedge \sim p$

Rewrite the following statements using the symbols of logic. Use p for the first statement, q for the second statement, and r (if necessary) for the third statement.

22. If you finish your homework, then you can go out tonight.

23. y is even or y is odd or y is even and odd.

24. Bill passed the test and Jill failed.

25. I will go to the movies if and only if you go with me.

26. If I go to work, then I will get paid and go to the bank.

Construct truth tables for the following problems:

27. $\sim p \vee \sim q$

28. $(p \rightarrow q) \Leftrightarrow (q \rightarrow p)$

29. $q \rightarrow (p \wedge \sim p)$

30. $q \rightarrow (p \vee \sim p)$

31. $(p \vee \sim p) \wedge \sim q$

32. $(p \vee q) \Leftrightarrow (\sim q \wedge \sim p)$

33. $[(p \rightarrow q) \wedge (q \rightarrow p)] \Leftrightarrow (p \Leftrightarrow q)$

Answers

1. Closed and true; 6 is even.

2. Open. Even if your weather forecast predicts rain tomorrow, you cannot be sure of the outcome.

3. Closed and true.

4. Open. Although the statement is true if x an y are positive as well as when x and y are negative, when they are of opposite signs the product is negative and the statement is not true.

5. Closed and false; 2 is even, and it is prime.

6. Open. The statement is dependent on when you are reading the passage.

7. Open. Since we don't know the value of x, we cannot say for sure if the statement is true or false.

8. All numbers greater than 5, or, written algebraically, $x > 5$. Solving the inequality by subtracting 3 from both sides gives the solution set.

9. All odd numbers greater than zero. Writing this in set notation, $\{1, 3, 5, 7, 9, \ldots\}$.

10. Washington. This could also be written in set notation, $\{$Washington$\}$.

11. The factors of a number are the numbers that divide into the number evenly, so the solution set of the factors of 28 would be $\{1, 2, 4, 7, 14, 28\}$.

12. y is even or y is odd.

13. If y is odd, then $y = 7$.

14. y is even or y is odd or $y = 7$.

15. y is even and y is not even.

16. $y = 7$ if and only if y is odd.

17. If y is even or y is odd, then $y = 7$.

18. If y is not even, then y is even.

19. y is not odd if and only if $y \neq 7$.

20. $y \neq 7$ and if y is even, then y is odd.

21. (y is not odd or $y = 7$) and y is not even.

22. Let p = "you finish your homework" and q = "you can go out tonight." The statement can then be rewritten as $p \rightarrow q$.

23. Let p = "y is even," q = "y is odd." The statement can then be rewritten as $p \vee q \vee (p \wedge q)$.

24. Let p = "Bill passed the test" and q = "Jill failed." The statement can then be rewritten as $p \wedge q$.

25. Let p = "I will go to the movies" and q = "you go with me." The statement can then be rewritten as $p \Leftrightarrow q$.

26. Let p = "I go to work," q = "I will get paid," and r = "I can go to the bank." Then the statement can be rewritten as $p \rightarrow q \wedge r$.

27. There will be columns for $\sim p$, $\sim q$, and for the final result. The last column will use the values of the 3rd and 4th columns to determine the final result.

p	q	$\sim p$	$\sim q$	$\sim p \vee \sim q$
T	T	F	F	F
T	F	F	T	T
F	T	T	F	T
F	F	T	T	T

28. First determine $p \rightarrow q$, then $q \rightarrow p$, then use both of these results for the final column.

p	q	$p \rightarrow q$	$q \rightarrow p$	$(p \rightarrow q) \Leftrightarrow (q \rightarrow p)$
T	T	T	T	T
T	F	F	T	F
F	T	T	F	F
F	F	T	T	T

29. First determine $\sim p$, then $p \wedge \sim p$, and then the final column.

p	q	$\sim p$	$p \wedge \sim p$	$q \rightarrow (p \wedge \sim p)$
T	T	F	F	F
T	F	F	F	T
F	T	T	F	F
F	F	T	F	T

30. The arrangement is similar to number 29, but with the 4th column as "or" instead of "and".

p	q	$\sim p$	$p \vee \sim p$	$q \rightarrow (p \vee \sim p)$
T	T	F	T	T
T	F	F	T	T
F	T	T	T	T
F	F	T	T	T

Problem 30 is a tautology.

31. First determine $\sim p$ and $\sim q$, then $p \vee \sim p$, and then the final column.

p	q	$\sim p$	$\sim q$	$p \vee \sim p$	$(p \vee \sim p) \wedge \sim q$
T	T	F	F	T	F
T	F	F	T	T	T
F	T	T	F	T	F
F	F	T	T	T	T

32. The first two columns will be for the negations of p and q. Then there will be columns for $p \vee q$ and $\sim q \wedge \sim p$, and finally, the final column.

p	q	$\sim p$	$\sim q$	$p \vee q$	$\sim q \wedge \sim p$	$(p \vee q) \Leftrightarrow (\sim q \wedge \sim p)$
T	T	F	F	T	F	F
T	F	F	T	T	F	F
F	T	T	F	T	F	F
F	F	T	T	F	T	F

33.

p	q	$p \rightarrow q$	$q \rightarrow p$	$(p \rightarrow q) \land (q \rightarrow p)$	$p \Leftrightarrow q$	$[(p \rightarrow q) \land (q \rightarrow p)] \Leftrightarrow (p \rightarrow q)$
T	T	T	T	T	T	T
T	F	F	T	F	F	T
F	T	T	F	F	F	T
F	F	T	T	T	T	T

Problem 33 is also a tautology.

Chapter 3

Algebra

A. Signed numbers

1. The rules for addition of signed numbers are as follows:

    In order to add two numbers with the same sign, add the absolute values of the numbers, and prefix the common sign to the result. In order to add two numbers with different signs, subtract the smaller absolute value from the larger absolute value; the sign of the result will be the sign of the number with the larger absolute value.

    Examples:

    $-3 + (-8) = -11$

    Both numbers are negative. We add the absolute values of the numbers and keep the negative sign for the answer.

    $4 + (-12) = -8$

    There is one positive and one negative number. Subtract the absolute value of the number with the smaller absolute value from the absolute value of the number with the larger absolute value ($12 - 4 = 8$) and keep the sign of the number with the larger absolute value. Since the absolute value of 12 is greater than the absolute value of 4, the sign of the answer will be negative.

    $-4 + 6 = 2$

    Again there is one positive and one negative number. Subtracting the absolute values of the two gives us an answer of 2. Since the absolute value of 6 is greater than the absolute value of 4, the answer is positive.

Subtraction can be thought of as the addition of the opposite. Change the subtraction sign to an addition sign and change the sign of the number which appears after the subtraction sign. Then you can use the rules of addition stated above.

$-3 - (-5) = 2$

Rewrite this problem as $-3 + 5$ by changing the subtraction sign to addition and changing the sign of negative 5 to positive 5.

$6 - 11 = -5$

Rewrite the phrase as $6 + (-11)$ and use the addition rules.

2. The rules for the multiplication and division of two signed numbers are identical. If both of the numbers are positive, the answer is positive. If both of the numbers are negative, multiply or divide as usual; the answer will be positive. If there is one positive and one negative number, then multiply or divide as usual; the answer will always be negative.

$(3)(-5) = -15$

One positive and one negative number will always give a negative answer when you multiply.

$(-4)(-2) = 8$

A negative number times a negative number always gives a positive number.

B. Basic properties of algebra

In order to understand and to work with variables, several concepts are needed.

The *commutative property* for addition and multiplication states that the order in which terms are combined is not important. $6 + 4$ is equal to $4 + 6$ and $(8)(5)$ is equivalent to $(5)(8)$.

The *associative property* for addition and multiplication states that the grouping of terms is not important. $(2 \cdot 3) \cdot 4$ is equal to $2 \cdot (3 \cdot 4)$ and $(5 + 6) + 1$ is equal to $5 + (6 + 1)$. Note that those properties do not hold for subtraction or division, however.

A third important property is the *distributive property* of multiplication. This property states that you can distribute a number you are multiplying by through terms being added or subtracted in parentheses. For example, 2(3 + 4) can be evaluated by distributing the 2 over both terms in the parentheses. So 2(3 + 4) is equivalent to 2(3) + 2(4).

The *order of operations* is the order in which computations should be performed in an expression which contains more than one operation. First, all work in parentheses is done. Then all exponents are evaluated. Third, all multiplications and divisions are performed from left to right in the expression, and lastly all additions and subtractions are performed from left to right in the expression.

Examples:

$9 - (3)(4)$ (multiply first)

$9 - 12$ (subtract)

-3

$-1.5\,[(4 - (-2.1)]^2$ (working inside parenthesis)

$-1.5(4 + 2.1)^2$ (add)

$-1.5(6.1)^2$ (exponents)

$-1.5(37.21)$ (multiplication)

-55.815

1. Variables

A variable is any symbol that stands for a number. We may not know the value of the variable. For example, let x stand for any number. Then we can write algebraic expressions involving this number x and perform operations on it. In order to be able to solve algebraic word problems, we will need to able to rewrite English phrases into algebraic ones.

English Phrase	Algebraic Phrase
the number	x
twice the number	$2x$
five more than the number	$x + 5$ (or $5 + x$)
three less than the number	$x - 3$
6 less than three times the number	$3x - 6$

2. Substitution

If we know the values of the variables in an algebraic expression, we can substitute those values for the variables and evaluate the expression.

Examples:

Let $x = 2$, $y = -3$, and $z = -4$. What is the value of $2x + 3y - z$?

$2x + 3y - z$

$2(2) + 3(-3) - (-4)$ by substitution

$4 + (-9) + 4$

$-5 + 4$

-1

The values of variables can also be substituted into formulas:

The area of a rectangle is defined by $A = lw$, where l is the length and w the width of the rectangle. What is the width of the rectangle when the length is 12 in. and the area is 198 sq. inches?

$A = lw$

$198 = 12w$

$16.5 = w$

The width is 16.5 in.

C. Polynomials

A *term* is defined to be any combination of variables and numbers connected by multiplication or division. Examples are $2x^2$, $.7xy^3$, and $-14xyz$. The number in front of the term is called the *coefficient*. x itself is a term with an implied coefficient of 1. Any whole number without a variable is called a *constant term*.

Combining terms via addition and subtraction forms expressions called *polynomials*. Certain polynomials have special names:

Name	Examples
monomials—one term	$3x$, 4, and $5w^4$
binomials—two terms	$3z + 1$, $x - y$, and $x^2 + 3x$
trinomials—three terms	$x^2 + 6x - 4$, and $4j^3 - d + 6q$

Like terms are terms that have exactly the same variables and exponents, such as $3x$ and $5x$ or $4z^2$ and $-9z^2$. Like terms can be added and subtracted, but terms which are not like cannot. To add or subtract like terms, add or subtract the coefficients and leave the common variables and exponents the same.

Examples:

$4x - 6x = -2x$
$3.5y^2 - 7.1y^2 = -3.6y^2$

Algebraic expressions can be simplified by combining all of the like terms the expression contains.

$3x - 4z + 6x - 10z = 9x - 14z$ (combining the $3x$ and $6x$ together and the $-4z$ and $-10z$ together)

When adding polynomials, rewrite the polynomials without the parentheses and gather like terms as before.

$(4x - 6) + (-3x - 8) =$
$4x - 6 + (-3x) - 8 = x - 14$

When subtracting polynomials, distribute the negative sign through the polynomial being subtracted. This changes the sign of every term inside the parentheses.

$(2r + 7) - (5r - 6) =$
$2r + 7 - 5r + 6$ (distributing the -1 changes $5r$ to $-5r$ and -6 to $+6$) $= 3r + 13$

1. Multiplication of monomials

    To multiply powers having the same base, use the rule for the multiplication of exponents:

    $$(x^a)(x^b) = x^{a+b}$$

    In other words, to multiply monomials, keep the base the same and add the exponents together.

    Examples:

    $(z^3)(z^5) = z^{3+5}$ or z^8

    $(x^2y^3)(x^4y^6) = x^6y^9$ (Add the exponents of 2 and 4 to obtain the new exponent for x, and add 3 and 6 to obtain the new exponent for y.)

    When coefficients are involved, multiply the coefficients as usual and use the exponent rule for the variables.

    $(3x^4)(5x^3) = 15x^7$ (Multiply the coefficients and add the exponents.)

    $(-3x^4z^2)(3x^2) = -9x^6z^2$

2. Multiplication of a Monomial by a Binomial

    To multiply a monomial by a binomial (or trinomial), combine the distributive property with the rules just learned for multiplying monomials. Distribute the monomial over the binomial, multiplying the coefficients and adding the exponents.

    Examples:

    $2x(x + 3) =$

    $\quad (2x)(x) + (2x)(3)$ (distributing the $2x$ over the binomial)

    $\quad 2x^2 + 6x$ (using the rules of multiplication)

    $4x^2y^2(3x^2 - 7y) =$

    $\quad (4x^2y^2)(3x^2) - (4x^2y^2)(7y)$ (distributing the $4x^2y^2$ over the binomial)

    $\quad 12x^4y^2 - 28x^2y^3$ (using the rules of multiplication)

$-3x^3(-2x^2 - 5x + 7) =$

$(-3x^3)(-2x^2) - (-3x^3)(5x) + (-3x^3)(7)$ (distributing the $-3x^3$ over the trinomial)

$6x^5 - (-15x^4) - 21x^3$ (using the rules of multiplication)

$6x^5 + 15x^4 - 21x^3$ (changing$-(-15x^4)$ to $+ 15x^4$)

3. Multiplying a binomial by another binomial

Students learn the acronym FOIL when they learn how to multiply binomials by binomials. FOIL stands for:

F—First terms in each parentheses, i.e., multiply the first term in the first pair of parentheses times the first term in the second pair of parentheses.

O—Outside terms, i.e., multiply the first term in the first pair of parentheses times the second term in the second pair of parentheses.

I—Inside terms, i.e., the second term in the first pair of parentheses times the first term in the second pair of parentheses.

L—The last terms in each pair of parentheses.

This memorization device indicates that binomials are multiplied by distributing the first term of the first binomial through the second pair of parentheses, and then distributing the second term of the first binomial through the second pair of parentheses.

Examples:

$(x + 5)(x - 3) =$

$(x)(x) - (x)(3) + (5)(x) - (5)(3)$ (FOIL or using the distributive property twice)

$x^2 - 3x + 5x - 15$ (multiplying the monomials)

$x^2 + 2x - 15$ (combining the like terms of $-3x$ and $5x$)

$(3x^2 - 2y)(2x^2 + 3y) =$

$(3x^2)(2x^2) + (3x^2)(3y) - (2y)(2x^2) - (2y)(3y)$ (using FOIL)

$6x^4 + 9x^2y - 4x^2y - 6y^2$ (multiplying monomials)

$6x^4 + 5x^2y - 6y^2$ (combining like terms)

The square of a binomial can also be computed by using FOIL.

$(2x - 3)^2$

$(2x - 3)(2x - 3)$ (rewriting without exponents)

$4x^2 - 6x - 6x + 9$ (FOIL)

$4x^2 - 12x + 9$ (combining like terms)

4. Division of monomials

In order to divide powers having the same base, subtract the exponents while keeping the base the same. If a variable does not have an exponent, it is assumed that the exponent is 1 (i.e., x is really x^1, but we rarely write an exponent of 1). The coefficients of the expression should be divided normally.
Stated algebraically:

$$\frac{x^a}{x^b} = x^{a-b}$$

Examples:

$\frac{x^6}{x^4} = x^{6-4} = x^2$ (keeping the base the same and subtracting the exponents)

$\frac{x^2y^3}{xy} = x^{2-1}y^{3-1} = x^1y^2$ or xy^2

5. Negative and zero exponents

By definition, a variable or constant raised to the zero power is equal to 1. This follows from our previous definition. $\frac{x^4}{x^4}$ should equal 1 since we are dividing equal quantities. But from our rule, $\frac{x^4}{x^4} = x^{4-4} = x^0$. So we define x^0 to be 1. Exponents can equal negative numbers as well. The definition of a negative exponent is as follows:

$$x^{-a} = \frac{1}{x^a}, a > 0$$

In other words, a variable with a negative exponent is equal to the reciprocal of that variable to the corresponding positive exponent. This again makes sense. If we are dividing $\frac{x^3}{x^7}$, then we should wind up with $\frac{1}{x^4}$ (the x^3 in the numerator canceling out 3 of the 7 x's in the denominator, leaving 4 x's, or x^4, in the denominator). Our definition of division of exponents would give us $\frac{x^3}{x^7} = x^{3-7} = x^{-4}$. Thus x^{-4} is defined to equal $\frac{1}{x^4}$.

Examples:

Evaluate $\frac{5^3}{5^6}$

5^{3-6} (rule for division with exponents

5^{-3}

$\frac{1}{5^3}$ (definition of a negative exponent)

$\frac{1}{125}$ (simplifying 5^3)

$\frac{8x^3}{2x^4} = 4x^{-1}$

which can also be written as $4\left(\frac{1}{x}\right)$ or $\frac{4}{x}$. (Notice that only the x, and not the 4, is being raised to a negative power, so only x is reciprocal and winds up in the denominator.)

$$\frac{16x^2y^3z}{-4xy^5z} =$$

$$\left(\frac{16}{-4}\right)(x^{2-1})\,(y^{3-5})\,(z^{1-1})\ \text{(dividing like bases)}$$

$$-4xy^{-2}z^0 \text{ or } \frac{-4x}{y^2}\ \text{(the } y^{-2} \text{ becomes a reciprocal and } z^0 = 1)$$

6. Factoring common factors

   Factoring is the process of rewriting a polynomial as the product of other polynomials. One method of factoring a polynomial is to remove ("factor out") the common factors from each term. These factors can be numbers or variables. Always try to factor out the greatest common factor. You may think of factoring out a common factor as "the distributive property in reverse."

   Examples:

   $6x - 8y$

   First, we determine the common factors of $6x$ and $8y$. The number 2 is a factor of both the $6x$ and the $8y$. Therefore divide both the $6x$ and $8y$ by the factor of 2, and put a 2 outside a set of parentheses.

   $$\frac{6x}{2} = 3x$$

   $$\frac{8y}{2} = 4y$$

   So, factoring $6x - 8y$ gives us $2(3x - 4y)$

   Note that this answer can be checked by using the distributive property to expand $2(3x - 4y)$.

   $10x^3 + 20x^2 + 10x$

   The greatest common factor is $10x$. Dividing each term by $10x$ gives $10x(x^2 + 2x + 1)$

   Certain trinomials can be factored into two binomials. Just as factoring out a common factor is the reverse of the distributive property, factoring a trinomial into two binomials is the reverse of the process of binomial multiplication (the FOIL method).

a. Factoring trinomials of the form $x^2 + bx + c$

When the coefficient of the squared term is 1, then you must find two numbers whose product is equal to c, the constant term, and whose sum is equal to b, the coefficient of the x term.

Examples:

Factor $x^2 + 5x + 6$

> 2 and 3 are the only two numbers whose product equals 6 and whose sum equals five. Thus the factorization is $(x + 2)(x + 3)$.

Note that you can FOIL to check your answer. Also note that the answer can have either binomial first, since multiplication is commutative. In other words, $(x + 3)(x + 2)$ is also a correct answer.

Factor $z^2 - 4z - 12$

> To factor this expression, find two numbers whose product is -12 and whose sum is -4.
> $(z - 6)(z + 2)$ is the answer, since -6 times 2 is -12 and -6 plus 2 is -4.

Factor $x^3 + 3x^2 - 18x$

> First, factor out the common factor of x.
> $x(x^2 + 3x - 18)$
> Now try to factor what remains in the parenthesis.
> $x(x + 6)(x - 3)$

Factor $y^2 - 4y + 7$

> There are no two numbers whose product is 7 and whose sum is -4. We say that this trinomial is "prime." A prime trinomial is one that cannot be factored.

b. Factoring trinomials of the form $ax^2 + bx + c$

Trinomials that have the form $ax^2 + bx + c$, where the coefficient of the squared term is not equal to one, can often be factored by a "brute force" approach. Find all the possible combinations of numbers that will multiply together to yield the squared term and all the possible combinations that multiply together to yield the constant term. Then test all possible variations to see which one will give you the middle term by FOIL.

Examples:

Factor $3x^2 + 10x - 8$

The factors of $3x^2$ can only be $3x$ and x, The factors of -8, however, can be 4 and -2, -4 and 2, 8 and -1, or -8 and 1. This means that the possible factorizations are:

$(3x + 4)(x - 2)$

$(3x - 2)(x + 4)$

$(3x - 4)(x + 2)$

$(3x + 2)(x - 4)$

$(3x + 8)(x - 1)$

$(3x - 1)(x + 8)$

$(3x - 8)(x + 1)$

$(3x + 1)(x - 8)$

The combinations must be tested until we find the combination which yields a middle term of $10x$.

$(3x + 4)(x - 2) = 3x^2 - 6x + 4x - 8 = 3x^2 - 2x - 8$ NO

$(3x - 2)(x + 4) = 3x^2 + 12x - 2x - 8 = 3x^2 + 10x - 8$ YES!!

So the answer is $(3x - 2)(x + 4)$

Factor $6x^2 - 19x + 15$

The factors of $6x^2$ are $6x$ and x, or $2x$ and $3x$. The factors of 15 are 5 and 3, -5 and -3, 1 and 15, or -1 and -15.

$(6x - 1)(x - 15) = 6x^2 - 90x - x + 15 = 6x^2 - 91x + 15$ NO

$(6x - 15)(x - 1) = 6x^2 - 6x - 15x + 15 = 6x^2 - 21x + 15$ NO

$(6x - 5)(x - 3) = 6x^2 - 18x - 5x + 15 = 6x^2 - 23x + 15$ NO

$(6x - 3)(x - 5) = 6x^2 - 30x - 3x + 15 = 6x^2 - 33x + 15$ NO

$$(2x - 1)(3x - 15) = 6x^2 - 30x - 3x + 15 = 6x^2 - 33x + 15 \qquad \text{NO}$$

$$(2x - 15)(3x - 1) = 6x^2 - 2x - 45x + 15 = 6x^2 - 47x + 15 \qquad \text{NO}$$

$$(2x - 5)(3x - 3) = 6x^2 - 6x - 15x + 15 = 6x^2 - 21x + 15 \qquad \text{NO}$$

$$(2x - 3)(3x - 5) = 6x^2 - 10x - 9x + 15 = 6x^2 - 19x + 15 \qquad \text{YES!}$$

So the answer is $(2x - 3)(3x - 5)$.

Note that to determine if a trinomial of this form is prime, you have to go through all the possibilities and test each one.

D. Solving equations

An equation is thought of as having two sides, separated by the equal sign. The key in algebra is to remember that whatever you do to one side of an equation, you must do to the other.

Solving an equation involves a process of inverting. The object is to get rid of all numbers on one side of the equation until only the variable remains. The lone number on the other side of the equation will be the answer, that is, the number that makes the equation a true one.

That process of inverting is accomplished by eliminating numbers on one side of an equation by performing the "opposite" operation to both sides of the equation. If a number is added to a variable, subtract it from both sides. If a number is subtracted from a variable, add it to both sides. If it is multiplied by the variable, divide it, and vice versa.

Examples:

Solve $x - 5 = 7$

Since 5 is being subtracted from the variable, do the opposite and add 5 to both sides. This will make the -5 cancel out on the left side leaving only the variable.

$$\begin{aligned} x - 5 &= 7 \\ +\,5 \quad & +5 \\ \hline x &= 12 \end{aligned}$$

Solve $\frac{y}{3} = 6$

Since the y is divided by 3, perform the opposite operation and multiply both sides by 3. This will cause the 3's on the left hand side of the equation to cancel.

$$\left(\frac{y}{3}\right)(3) = 6(3)$$

$$y = 18$$

Solve $3x - 2 = 7$

Get rid of -2 on the left side by adding 2 to both sides.

$$
\begin{array}{rcr}
3x - 2 & = & 7 \\
+ 2 & & +2 \\
\hline
3x & = & 9
\end{array}
$$

Now divide both sides by 3 to undo the multiplication by 3

$$\frac{3x}{3} = \frac{9}{3}$$

$$x = 3$$

Solve $-18 = 3x + 4$

$$
\begin{array}{rcl}
-4 & & -4 \text{ (subtracting 4 to get rid of the } +4 \text{ on the right)} \\
\hline
-22 & = & 3x
\end{array}
$$

$$\frac{-22}{3} = \frac{3x}{3} \quad \text{(dividing both sides by 3)}$$

$$\frac{-22}{3} = x$$

Solve $\dfrac{3x}{5} = 6$

With fractional coefficients, sometimes it's quicker to multiply both sides by the reciprocal of the fraction. This has the same effect as dividing by the fraction.

$$\left(\frac{5}{3}\right)\left(\frac{3}{5}\right)x = \left(\frac{5}{3}\right)(6)$$

$$x = 10$$

Sometimes, you have to combine like terms together first.

Solve $2y - 6 = 4y + 3$

Now there is a choice. We can either move the $4y$ over to the left side to combine with the $2y$, by subtracting $4y$ from both sides, or we can move the $2y$ over to the same side as the $4y$, by subtracting $2y$ from both sides. Either way we will end up with the same answer.

$$
\begin{array}{rcl}
2y - 6 &=& 4y + 3 \\
-4y & & -4y \\
\hline
-2y - 6 &=& 3 \\
 & & +6 \quad +6 \\
\hline
-2y &=& 9 \\
\dfrac{-2y}{-2} &=& \dfrac{9}{-2} \\
y &=& \dfrac{-9}{2}
\end{array}
$$

E. Solving inequalities

Solving inequalities involves the same rules as solving equations, but there is one additional rule. If you multiply or divide both sides of an inequality by a negative number, then the sign of the inequality must be switched. For example, if the sign in an inequality problem is $>$ and you multiply both sides of this inequality by -3, then the inequality sign will change to $<$.

Examples:

Solve $3x - 5 > 4$

$$\underline{+5 \ +5} \quad \text{(adding 5 to both sides to get rid of the minus 5)}$$
$$3x > 9$$

$$\frac{3x}{3} > \frac{9}{3} \quad \text{(dividing both sides by 3)}$$
$$x > 3$$

Solve $-2x - 6 \leq 4$ (the inequality sign switches since we divided by a negative number)

$$\underline{+6 \ +6}$$

$$-2x \leq 10$$

$$\frac{-2x}{-2} \geq \frac{10}{-2}$$
$$x \geq -5$$

You can also graph your answer on the number line. If the inequality is of the form $x < a$ or $x > a$, begin by making an open circle at a. If the inequality is of the form $x \leq a$ or $x \geq a$, begin by making a closed circle at a. You then shade to the right or left of a, depending on the direction of the inequality. For example, if you were to graph $x > 5$, you would put an open circle on 5 and shade all values greater than 5, that is, all numbers to the right of 5 on the number line.

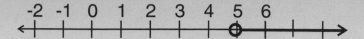

In order to graph $y \leq 2$, you would put a closed circle on 2, and then shade everything to the left of 2, indicating all values less than 2.

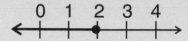

F. Solving quadratic equations

There is a special technique for solving a quadratic equation. The method is based on the concept that if there are two numbers, A and B, and A times B equals 0, then it must be true that either $A = 0$ or $B = 0$.

To solve a quadratic equation, begin by rewriting it in the form $ax^2 + bx + c = 0$. Then, factor the left hand side, and set each factor individually equal to zero.

Examples

$x^2 - 5x = 6$

$x^2 - 5x - 6 = 0$ (subtracting 6 from both sides to collect all terms on the same side of the equation)

$(x - 6)(x + 1) = 0$ (factoring $x^2 - 5x - 6$)

$x - 6 = 0$ or $x + 1 = 0$ (If $AB = 0$, then $A = 0$ or $B = 0$.)

$x = 6$ or $x = -1$

G. Ratio and Proportion

A *ratio* is a comparison of any two numbers. Ratios are often written as fractions or numbers separated by a colon. For example, the ratio of 35 miles for every 2 gallons of gas can be written as $\frac{35}{2}$ or 35:2. A *proportion* is an equation containing two ratios set equal to each other. A proportion is solved by a process called *cross multiplying*, where the product of the upper left number and the lower right number is set equal to the product of the lower left number and the upper right number.

For example, consider the proportion $\frac{a}{b} = \frac{c}{d}$. Cross multiplying gives the equation $ad = bc$.

We give special names to the components of this cross product. a and d are called the extremes, and b and c are called the means. Thus the product of the means is equal to the product of the extremes.

Examples:

Solve $\frac{4}{x} = \frac{6}{4}$

Since the product of the means equals the product of the extremes, we can cross multiply and get the equation:

$6x = 16$

$x \approx 2.7$ (by dividing both sides by 6)

If a dozen doughnuts cost $3.60, then how much will 20 doughnuts cost?

Set up the problem as a proportion, with the first clause in the problem yielding the ratio $\frac{12}{3.60}$. The second ratio must have the same two units in the same two places $\left(\frac{\text{\# of doughnuts}}{\text{cost}} \right)$, so that ratio would be $\frac{20}{x}$. Now we can set up the proportion and solve.

$\frac{12}{3.6} = \frac{20}{x}$

$12x = 72$

$x = 6$

20 doughnuts cost $6.

Two numbers have a sum of 848, and they are in the ratio of 3:5. What are the numbers?

The fact that the ratio is 3:5 means that there is a number x such that the two numbers are $3x$ and $5x$. Thus $3x + 5x = 848$.

$8x = 848$

$x = 106$

If $x = 106$, then the numbers are $3(106) = 318$ and $5(106) = 530$.

H. Radicals

A square root of a number a, is defined as a number with the property that, when it is squared, the result is a. For example, 25 has 2 square roots, 5 and -5. $5^2 = 25$ and $(-5^2) = 25$. By convention, the radical symbol $\sqrt{}$ refers to the positive square root. For example, $\sqrt{16} = 4$. In this section we are only concerned with some basic rules of radicals.

Radicals can be multiplied or divided by using the following rules:

$$\sqrt{x}\sqrt{y} = \sqrt{xy} \text{ and } \frac{\sqrt{x}}{\sqrt{y}} = \sqrt{\frac{x}{y}}$$

Radicals can be added or subtracted only if they are "like," that is, if they have same number under the radical sign. For example, $3\sqrt{5} + 8\sqrt{5} = 11\sqrt{5}$, but $\sqrt{7} + \sqrt{3}$ cannot be written in a simpler form.

The above rules can be used to simplify radicals, as the examples below show.

Examples:

Simplify $\sqrt{125}$

> Look for a perfect square that will divide into 125 evenly. Twenty-five will work, since 25 goes into 125 evenly. So
>
> $$\sqrt{125} = \sqrt{25 \cdot 5} = \sqrt{25}\sqrt{5} = 5\sqrt{5}$$

Simplify $3\sqrt{7} + 5\sqrt{7}$

> Since the radicals are like, the radicals can be combined. To do this, add the coefficients and keep the number under the radical symbol the same.
>
> $$3\sqrt{7} + 5\sqrt{7} = (3 + 5)\sqrt{7} = 8\sqrt{7}$$

Questions

1. $-4 + (-6) + (-7) =$

2. $(-.4)(-.3)(-.2) =$

3. $-8 - 9 + 4 - (-3) =$

State what property is being used in each example

4. $(-6)(9) = (9)(-6)$

5. $2(x + 5) = (2)(x) + (2)(5)$

Simplify:

6. $3 + 9 \cdot 7 - \frac{16}{2}$

7. $3 - 4(5 - 2)$

8. $\frac{7 \cdot 2 + 2 \cdot 5^2}{13 - 4 - 1}$

If x is the missing number, write an algebraic phrase for these English phrases.

9. Three less than the number

10. Eight times a number

11. One fourth of a number

12. Seven decreased by three times a number

13. Six times the positive difference of a number greater than five and five

Substitution: Let $x = -5$, $y = 4$, and $z = -3$. Find:

14. $y^2 - x^2$

15. $3z^2 + 2x^2$

Let $a = -3$, $b = -2$, $c = 5$, and $d = 2$. Find:

16. $ab + cd$

17. $abcd$

18. $a^2 + b^2$

19. $(3a - 2) + (4a + 7)$

Simplify:

20. $(4x - 3) - (x + 7)$

21. $(x + 7) - (x + 3) + (x + 4)$

22. $x^4 x^2 x$

23. $(5x^3)(-.2x^2)$

24. $(-3x^2y)(-4xy)(-3x^2y^3)$

25. $(-4x^2)(x^2)(-3x)(x^3)(-x)(-2x^2)$

Multiply:

26. $(y + 3)(y + 5)$

27. $(x - 3)(x - 4)$

28. $(3x - 1)^2$

29. $(9z - 4y)(3z + y)$

Simplify:

30. 4^{-2}

31. $\dfrac{16\,x^5}{8x^3}$

32. $\dfrac{24\,x^2y^3z^4}{12x^3yz^6}$

Factor:

33. $4x + 8y - 16$

34. $4y^3 - 8y^2$

35. $10y^3 - 5y^2 - 5y$

Factor completely:

36. $x^2 + 2x - 15$

37. $y^2 + y - 12$

38. $8y^3 + 8y^2 + 2y$

39. $3z^2 - 11z + 10$

Solve these equations:

40. $y - 7 = 14$

41. $\dfrac{1}{2}x = 17$

42. $3x + 4 + 2x - 5 = 0$

Solve and graph your solution.

43. $x + 7 > 14$

44. $\dfrac{3}{4}y \le -12$

45. $x - 3 < 3x - 1$

Solve:

46. $x^2 + 7x + 6 = 0$

47. $x^2 + 10x = -25$

48. $6x^2 = 5x + 6$

Solve the proportions:

49. $\dfrac{x}{5} = \dfrac{3}{4}$

50. $\dfrac{6}{x} = 7$

51. $\dfrac{4}{x + 1} = \dfrac{x + 1}{x}$

Solve:

52. If 4 jars of honey cost $7.20, then how much would 7 jars cost?

53. A recipe for 3 dozen cookies calls for 600g of flour to be used. How many cookies can I make with 900g of flour?

54. Two numbers are in the ratio of 5:4 and their total is 558. What are the numbers?

57

Simplify:

55. $(4 \sqrt{6})(5 \sqrt{8})$

56. $(3 - \sqrt{11})(3 + \sqrt{11})$

Solve. Remember the Pythagorean Theorem: $(c^2 = a^2 + b^2)$.

57. A ladder 20 ft. tall is resting against a wall. If the ladder is touching the wall 15 ft. up, then how far away from the wall is the bottom of the ladder?

58. If the two legs of a right triangle are 12 in. and 5 in., then how long is the hypotenuse?

Answers

1. $-4 + (-6) + (-7) = -17$. Since all the numbers are negative, add the three together and keep the answer negative.

2. $(-.4)(-.3)(-.2) =$

   $(.12)\,(-.2) =$ (negative times
   $-.024$ negative is positive)
                      (positive times
                      negative is negative)

3. $-8 - 9 + 4 - (-3) =$

   $-8 + (-9) + 4 + 3 =$ (rewriting the
   $-17 + 4 + 3 =$ subtraction parts as
   $-13 + 3 =$ adding the opposite)
   -10

4. $(-6)(9) = (9)(-6)$

   The commutative property. The order is changed.

5. $2(x + 5) = (2)(x) + (2)(5)$

   The distributive property. The 2 is distributed through multiplication through every term in the parentheses.

6. $3 + 9 \cdot 7 - \dfrac{16}{2} =$

   $3 + 63 - 8 =$ (multiplication and division first)
   $66 - 8 =$
   58

7. $(3 - 4)(5 - 2) =$

   $3 - 4 \cdot 3 =$
   $3 - 12 =$
   $3 + (-12) =$
   -9

8. $\dfrac{7 \cdot 2 + 2 \cdot 5^2}{13 - 4 - 1} =$

   $\dfrac{7 \cdot 2 + 2 \cdot 25}{8} =$

   $\dfrac{14 + 50}{8} =$

   $\dfrac{64}{8} =$

   8

9. $x - 3$

10. $8x$

11. $\left(\dfrac{1}{4}\right)x$

12. $7 - 3x$

13. $6(x - 5)$

14. $y^2 - x^2$

   $(4)^2 - (-5)^2 =$ (substituting 4 for y
                      and -5 for x)
   $16 - 25 =$
   -9

15. $3z^2 + 2x^2$

$3(-3)^2 + 2(-5)^2 =$
$3(9) + 2(25) =$
$27 + 50 =$
77

16. $ab + cd$

$(-3)(-2) + (5)(2) =$
$6 + 10 =$
16

17. $abcd$

$(-3)(-2)(5)(2) =$
60

18. $a^2 + b^2$

$(-3)^2 + (-2)^2 =$
$9 + 4 =$
13

19. $(3a - 2) + (4a + 7)$

$3a + 4a - 2 + 7$ (rearranging terms)
$7a + 5$ (combining like terms)
$7(-3) + 5 = -21 + 5 = -16$

20. $(4x - 3) - (x + 7) =$

$4x - 3 - x - 7 =$
$3x - 10$

21. $(x + 7) - (x + 3) + (x + 4) =$

$(x + 7) - x - 3 + (x + 4) = x + 8$

22. $x^4 x^2 x =$

$x^{4+2+1} =$ (remember $x = x^1$)
x^7

23. $(5x^3)(-.2x^2) =$

$(5)(-.2)(x^3)(x^2) =$
$-1x^5$ or $-x^5$

24. $(-3x^2y)(-4xy)(-3x^2y^3) =$

$(-3)(-4)(-3)(x^2)(x)(x^2)(y)(y)(y^3) =$
$-36x^5y^5$

25. $(-4x^2)(x^2)(-3x)(x^3)(-x)(-2x^2) =$

$(-4)(-3)(-1)(-2)(x^2)(x^2)(x)(x^3)(x)(x^2) =$
$24x^{11}$

26. $(y + 3)(y + 5) =$

$(y)(y) + (5)(y) + (3)(y) + (3)(5)$ (FOIL) $=$
$y^2 + 5y + 3y + 15 =$
$y^2 + 8y + 15$ (combining the like
                          terms $5y$ and $3y$)

27. $(x - 3)(x - 4) =$

$x^2 - 4x - 3x + 12$ (FOIL) $=$
$x^2 - 7x + 12$ (combining like terms)

28. $(3x - 1)^2$

Remember, $(3x - 1)^2$ really means

$(3x - 1)(3x - 1) =$
$9x^2 - 3x - 3x + 1 =$
$9x^2 - 6x + 1$

29. $(9z - 4y)(3z + y) =$

$27z^2 + 9yz - 12yz - 4y^2 =$
$27z^2 - 3yz - 4y^2$

30. $4^{-2} =$

   $\dfrac{1}{4^2}$ (definition of a negative exponent) $=$

   $\dfrac{1}{16}$

31. $\dfrac{16x^5}{8x^3} =$

   $\left(\dfrac{16}{8}\right)\left(\dfrac{x^5}{x^3}\right) =$

   $2(x^{5-3}) =$

   $2x^2$

32. $\dfrac{24\,x^2y^3z^4}{12x^33yz^6} =$

   $\left(\dfrac{24}{12}\right)\left(\dfrac{x^2}{x^3}\right)\left(\dfrac{y^3}{y}\right)\left(\dfrac{z^4}{z^6}\right) =$

   $2x^{-1}y^2z^{-2}$ or $\dfrac{2y^2}{xz^2}$

33. $4x + 8y - 16$

   Finding a common factor of 4 in each term:
   $4(x + 2y - 4)$ (dividing each term by 4)

34. $4y^3 - 8y^2 =$

   $4y^2(y - 2)$ (remember there are other
   factors to divide by, but $4y^2$
   is the greatest common
   factor to use)

35. $10y^3 - 5y^2 - 5y =$

   $5y(2y^2 - y - 1) =$
   $5y(2y + 1)(y - 1)$

36. $x^2 + 2x - 15 =$

   $(x + 5)(x - 3)$ (5 and -3 multiply to -15
   and add to 2)

37. $y^2 + y - 12 =$

   $(y + 4)(y - 3)$ (4 times -3 gives -12
   and 4 plus -3 gives 1)

38. $8y^3 + 8y^2 + 2y$

   First, look for the largest common factor.

   $2y(4y^2 + 4y + 1)$

   Now factor what is in parentheses.

   $2y(2y + 1)(2y + 1)$
   or $2y(2y + 1)^2$

39. $3z^2 - 11z + 10$

   Factors of $3z^2$: $3z$ and z
   Factors of 10: 5 and 2, -5 and -2
   The combination that works is
   $(3z - 5)(z - 2)$

40. $y - 7 = 14$

   $\underline{ + 7 + 7}$ (adding 7 to both sides
   to get rid of the -7)

   $y = 21$

41. $\dfrac{1}{2}x = 17$

   $(2)(\dfrac{1}{2})\,x = (2)(17)$ (multiplying both
   sides by the
   reciprocal of $\dfrac{1}{2}$)

   $x = 34$

42. $3x + 4 + 2x - 5 = 0$

$5x - 1 = 0$ (Since the like terms are on the same side of the equation, I can add them together without having to add or subtract them to the other side of the equation.)

$5x \quad - 1 = 0$

$\underline{\qquad + 1 + 1}$

$5x \qquad = 1$

$\dfrac{5x}{5} = \dfrac{1}{5}$

$x = \dfrac{1}{5} \text{ or } .2$

43. $x + 7 > 14$

$- 7 - 7$

$x > 7$ \qquad (Subtraction does not change the inequality sign.)

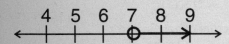

44. $\dfrac{3}{4} y \leq -12$

$\left(\dfrac{4}{3}\right)\left(\dfrac{3}{4}\right) y \leq \left(\dfrac{4}{3}\right)(-12)$

$y \leq -16$

45. \qquad $x - 3 \; < \; 3x - 1$

$\underline{\qquad -3x \qquad \quad - 3x}$

$-2x - 3 \; < -1$

$\underline{\qquad + 3 \qquad +3}$

$-2x \; < \quad 2$

$\dfrac{-2x}{-2} > \dfrac{2}{-2}$

$x > -1$

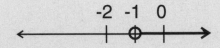

46. $x^2 + 7x + 6 = 0$

$(x + 6)(x + 1)$ (factoring the quadratic)

$x + 6 = 0 \text{ or } x + 1 = 0$

$x = -6 \text{ or } x = -1$

47. $x^2 + 10x = -25$

$x^2 + 10x + 25 = 0$

$(x + 5)(x + 5) = 0$

$x + 5 = 0 \text{ or } x + 5 = 0$

$x = -5 \text{ or } x = -5$

The only solution to this equation is -5. This is called a double root.

48. $6x^2 = 5x + 6$

$6x^2 - 5x - 6 = 0$

$(2x - 3)(3x + 2) = 0$

$2x - 3 = 0 \text{ or } 3x + 2 = 0$

$2x = 3 \text{ or } 3x = -2$

$x = \dfrac{3}{2} \text{ or } x = \dfrac{-2}{3}$

49. $\frac{x}{5} = \frac{3}{4}$

$15 = 4x$ (the product of the means equals the product of the extremes)

$3.75 = x$

50. $\frac{6}{x} = 7$

$\frac{6}{x} = \frac{7}{1}$ (rewriting 7 as $\frac{7}{1}$ to have a proportion)

$7x = 6$ (cross products)

$x = \frac{6}{7}$

51. $\frac{4}{x+1} = \frac{x+1}{x}$

$(x+1)(x+1) = 4x$

$x^2 + 2x + 1 = 4x$

$x^2 - 2x + 1 = 0$

$(x-1)(x-1) = 0$

$x - 1 = 0$ or $x - 1 = 0$

$x = 1$ or $x = 1$

52. $\frac{4}{7.2} = \frac{7}{x}$

$50.4 = 4x$ (cross multiplying)

$12.6 = x$

7 jars would cost $12.60

53. $\frac{3}{600} = \frac{x}{900}$

$600x = 2,700$ (cross multiplying)

$x = 4.5$

4.5 dozen cookies or 54 cookies

54. $5x + 4x = 558$

$9x = 558$

$x = 62$

The numbers are 5(62) and 4(62), or 310 and 248

55. $(4\sqrt{6})(5\sqrt{8})$

$20\sqrt{48}$ (multiplying radicals)

$20\sqrt{(16)(3)}$

$20\sqrt{16}\sqrt{3}$ $(\sqrt{ab} = \sqrt{a}\sqrt{b})$

$80\sqrt{3}$ (since $\sqrt{16} = 4$)

56. $(3 - \sqrt{11})(3 + \sqrt{11}) =$

$9 + 3\sqrt{11} - 3\sqrt{11} - (\sqrt{11})^2$ (FOIL)

$= 9 - (\sqrt{11})^2$ (combining like radicals)

$= 9 - 11$ (simplifying radicals)

$= -2$

57. The ladder is the hypotenuse of the right triangle, and the 15 would be one of its legs. So, using the Pythagorean Theorem

$c^2 = a^2 + b^2$

$20^2 = a^2 + 15^2$

$400 = a^2 + 225$

$175 = a^2$ (subtracting 225 from both sides)

$5\sqrt{7} = a$

58. $c^2 = a^2 + b^2$

$c^2 = 12^2 + 5^2$

$c^2 = 144 + 25$

$c^2 = 169$

$c = 13$ (by taking the positive square root of both sides)

Chapter 4

Geometry

A. Undefined terms

Geometry begins with a groundwork of three undefined terms upon which everything else is built. These terms are *point, line,* and *plane.* Intuitively, a plane is a two-dimensional flat surface. A point is an infinitely small dot. A line is a group of these points extending outward infinitely in two directions.

You should be familiar with the following definitions:

B. Lines

1. *Parallel lines*—Lines that are always the same distance from each other. If two lines are not parallel, we say that they are intersecting lines.

2. *Perpendicular lines*—Lines that cross at a 90 degree angle. Perpendicularity is designated by a little box drawn at the intersection of the lines.

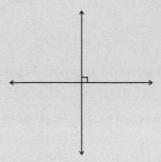

3. *Transversal*—A line that intersects two (or more) lines.

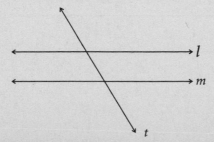

t is a transversal of lines *l* and *m.*

C. Angles

1. *acute angle*—an angle measuring less than 90 degrees

2. *obtuse angle*—an angle whose measure is greater than 90 degrees but less than 180 degrees

3. *right angle*—an angle whose measure is exactly 90 degrees

4. *straight angle*—an angle whose measure is exactly 180 degrees (a straight line)

5. *complementary angles*—two angles whose measures total 90 degrees

6. *supplementary angles*—two angles whose measures total 180 degrees

7. *vertical angles*—corresponding angles formed by two intersecting lines. These angles always have the same measure.

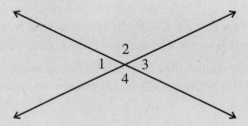

In the above figure, angles 1 and 3 are vertical angles. Angles 2 and 4 are also vertical angles.

The diagram below depicts two parallel lines cut by a transversal.

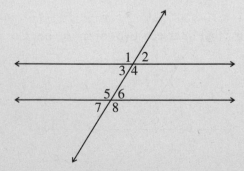

Note that eight angles are formed when the transversal cuts the parallel lines.

8. *corresponding angles*—corresponding angles are angles that correspond to the same position when 2 lines are cut by a transversal. For example, angle 2 and angle 6 are corresponding angles in the figure above, since each angle is in the upper right. Angle 1 and angle 5 are also corresponding, since each is in the upper left. Angle 3 and angle 7 are corresponding, as are angle 4 and angle 8. When parallel lines are cut by a transversal, the corresponding angles are equal.

9. *alternate interior angles*—when two lines are cut by a transversal, alternate interior angles are angles that are on opposite sides of the transversal and are between the two lines. Angle 3 and 6 are alternate angles. Angles 4 and 5 are as well. When two parallel lines are cut by a transversal, the alternate interior angles are equal.

10. *alternate exterior angles*—These pairs of angles are on opposite sides of the transversal, and are on the "outside" of the lines. In the figure above, angle 1 and angle 8 are alternate exterior angles, as are angles 2 and 7. When two parallel lines are cut by a transversal, the alternate exterior angles are equal.

Examples:

Find the missing measures in the following figures.

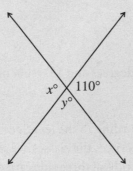

In the figure above, the angles labeled $x°$ and $110°$ are vertical angles, so $x° = 110°$ as well. The angles labeled $110°$ and $y°$ are supplementary, so $y° = 180° - 110° = 70°$.

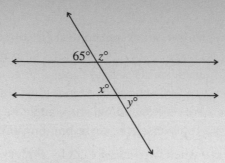

In this figure, the angles labeled $x°$ and $65°$ are corresponding angles, and thus have the same measure. The angles labeled $y°$ and $65°$ are alternate exterior angles and have the same measure. The angles labeled $z°$ and $65°$ are supplementary so $z°$ = $180° - 65° = 115°$.

The measure of the complement of an angle is 60 degrees more than the angle. What are the measures of the two angles?

> Let x be the measure of one angle. Its complement would measure $x + 60$.
>
> $x + x + 60 = 90$ (complementary angles add up to 90 degrees).
>
> $2x + 60 = 90$
>
> $2x = 30$
>
> $x = 15$

So the angles measure 15 degrees and 15 + 60, or 75 degrees.

D. Triangles

Triangles can be classified according to the length of their sides or the measure of their angles. As far as sides are concerned, the classes are *scalene* (no sides equal), *isosceles* (two sides equal), and *equilateral* (all three sides are equal). As for angles, the classes are *acute* (all angles under 90 degrees), *right* (one 90 degree angle), and *obtuse* (one angle over 90 degrees).

The theorems you need to know about triangles are as follows:

1. The sum of the measures of the three angles in a triangle is always 180 degrees.

2. The measure of an exterior angle of a triangle (the angle formed by extending a side of the triangle) is equal to the sum of the measures of the two "remote interior" angles in the triangle. That is, in triangle *ABC* below, the measure of angle 4 will be equal to the sum of the measures of angles 2 and 3.

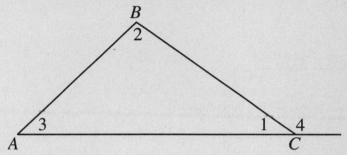

3. The Pythagorean Theorem was already mentioned in the algebra chapter in question 57 on page 45. It states that the sum of the squares of the legs of a right triangle will be equal to the square of the hypotenuse. The hypotenuse is the longest side, that is, the side opposite the 90 degree angle.

    $c^2 = a^2 + b^2$

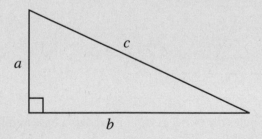

4. The base angles of an isosceles triangle are of equal measure. The base angles of an isosceles triangle are the angles opposite the two sides of equal length.

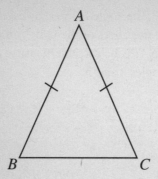

Angle *B* and angle *C* are the base angles.

5. The area formula for a triangle is $A = \frac{1}{2}\,bh$, where b = the length of the base of the triangle and h = the length of the height drawn to the base.

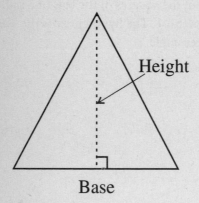

Note that in right triangles the two legs can be used as a base and height of the triangle.

Examples:

The measures of the base angles of an isosceles triangle are 30 degrees less than the measure of the other angle. What are the measures of all three angles?

Call the degree measure of the base angles of the triangle *x*. Then the third angle will have a degree measure of *x* + 30. The three angles then measure *x* degrees, *x* degrees, and *x* + 30 degrees. Since the sum of the measures of the angles of a triangle is 180 degrees, we get the equation:

$x + x + x + 30 = 180$

$3x + 30 = 180$

$3x = 150$

$x = 50$

So the angle measurements are 50, 50, and 80 degrees.

The third side of an isosceles triangle is 5 cm more than either of the other two sides. If the perimeter of the triangle is 26 cm, what are the lengths of the other two sides?

Let x be the length of one of the two equal sides. The longer side will be $x + 5$.

$x + x + (x + 5) = 26$ (perimeter is the sum of all 3 sides)

$3x + 5 = 26$

$3x = 21$

$x = 7$

So the lengths of the sides are 7 cm, 7 cm, and $7 + 5$, or 12 cm.

E.   Quadrilaterals

Quadrilaterals are four sided figures. There are many classifications of quadrilaterals. The most important ones are as follows:

1.   *Parallelogram*—Has opposite sides that are parallel and congruent. Its opposite angles are congruent as well.

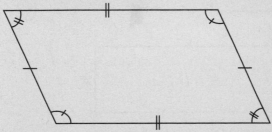

2.   *Rectangle*—A parallelogram with the additional property that its angles are right angles. The diagonals of a rectangle are congruent.

3.   *Rhombus*—A parallelogram with the additional property that its sides are equal.

4. *Square*—A quadrilateral with four equal sides and four equal angles. It has all of the properties of the parallelogram and the rhombus.

5. *Trapezoid*—A quadrilateral with one pair of parallel sides.

    Note that the sum of the angles of any quadrilateral is always 360 degrees.

Area formulas:

Square is: $A = s^2$, where s is the length of a side of the square.

Rectangle: $A = lw$, where l is the length and w the width of the rectangle.

Parallelogram: $A = bh$ where b is the length of the base and h is the height.

Trapezoid: $A = \left(\dfrac{1}{2}\right)h(b_1 + b_2)$ where h is the height of the trapezoid and b_1 and b_2 are the lengths of the two parallel bases.

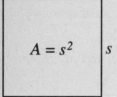

$$A = s^2 \qquad s$$

$$A = lw \qquad w$$

$$l$$

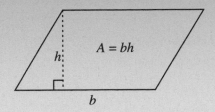

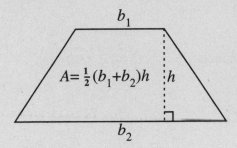

Perimeter formulas:

Square: $P = 4s$

Rectangle: $P = 2l + 2w$

Examples:

What is the perimeter and area of a rectangle whose dimensions are 5 m by 12 m?

Let the length of the rectangle be 12 m and the width be 5 m.

$A = lw$

$A = (12)(5)$

$A = 60$ m^2 (m^2 stands for square meters. All areas are expressed in square units.)

$P = 2l + 2w$

$P = 2(12) + 2(5)$

$P = 24 + 10$

$P = 34$ m

The length of a rectangle is 3 m less than twice the width. Its perimeter is 48 m. Find the length and width of the rectangle.

If x is the width of the rectangle, then $2x - 3$ represents the length.

$2l + 2w = P$ (perimeter formula for a rectangle)

$2(2x - 3) + 2(x) = 48$ (substitution)

$4x - 6 + 2x = 48$

$6x - 6 = 48$

$6x = 54$

$x = 9$

The width is 9 m, and the length is $2(9) - 3 = 15$ m.

F.   Circles

Basic Vocabulary and formulas

1.   *Radius*—the distance from the center of a circle to any point on the circle

2.   *Diameter*—a line segment that goes from one point on the circle to another and also passes through its center. It cuts the circle in two congruent halves.

3.   *pi* (π)—The ratio of the circumference of a circle to its diameter. Pi is an irrational number (i.e., a number that can be expressed only as a nonterminating, nonrepeating decimal), and so we use different approximations for pi, depending on how accurate we want to be. Some of the more common approximations are 3.14 and the fraction $\frac{22}{7}$.

4.   *Circumference*—the distance around the circle. The formula for circumference is $C = 2\pi r$ or $C = \pi d$, where r is the radius and d is the diameter.

5.   The area formula for a circle is $A = \pi r^2$ where r is the radius.

Examples:

Find the area of the figures below. Use $\pi = 3.14$.

1.

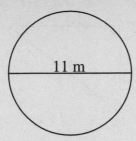

2.

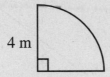

In problem 1, the diameter is 11 m, which we have to divide by two to find the radius. Then we substitute the radius in the formula $A = \pi r^2$

$A = (3.14)(5.5)^2$

$A = (3.14)(30.25)$

$A = 94.985 \text{ m}^2$

In problem 2, since we are given only a quarter circle, we will find the area of the entire circle and then divide it by four.

$A = \pi r^2$

$A = (3.14)(4)^2$

$A = (3.14)(16)$

$A = 50.24 \text{ m}^2$

But, that is the area of the entire circle, so the final answer is

$\frac{50.24}{4} = 12.56 \text{ m}^2.$

G. Similar figures

Similar figures are ones whose corresponding angles are congruent, and whose sides are in proportion to each other.

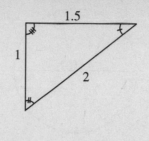

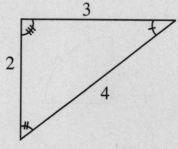

In the two triangles above, the angle measures are the same and the ratio of corresponding sides is the same at 2:1. Therefore, these two triangles are similar.

Examples:

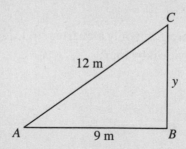

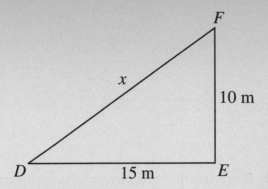

Given that the following two triangles are similar, with $\angle A = \angle D$, $\angle B = \angle E$, and $\angle C = \angle F$ find the lengths of the missing sides.

From sides *AB* and *DE*, we can find the ratio between the corresponding sides of these similar figures. The ratio is 9:15 (or 3:5). This becomes the first ratio in a proportion to solve for the missing sides.

$$\frac{3}{5} = \frac{y}{10}$$

$$5y = 30$$

$$y = 6 \text{ m}$$

$$\frac{3}{5} = \frac{12}{x}$$

$$60 = 3x$$

$$20 \text{ m} = x$$

H. Solids

The three dimensional shapes you need to know about are *prisms, pyramids, cylinders, cones,* and *spheres.* Prisms are a general category of figures which have a face of a two dimensional object (square, triangle, etcetera) and are "stretched" into three dimensions. Some examples are:

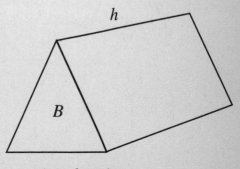

triangular prism

77

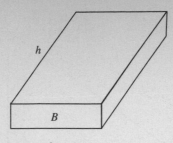

rectangular prism

We use the formula $V = Bh$ to find the volume of prisms. B stands for the area of the base, and h stands for the height, or how far this shape has been "stretched" into three dimensions.

The volume formula for the cylinder is derived the same way. Find the area of the circular base and multiply by its height. $V = \pi r^2 h$

Pyramids and cones have a volume formula of $V = \left(\frac{1}{3}\right) Bh$, where once again B stands for the area of the base, and h is the height.

Spheres have a volume given by the formula $V = \frac{4}{3} \pi r^3$, where r is the radius.

Examples:

Find the volume of the following figures: Let $\pi = 3.14$.

1.

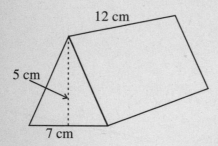

2.

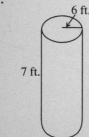

78

3.

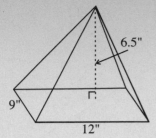

6.5"

9"

12"

In figure 1, we have a triangular prism. First we figure out the area of the triangle. This will be B in our volume formula.

$$A = \left(\frac{1}{2}\right)bh$$

$$A = \left(\frac{1}{2}\right)(5)(7)$$
$$A = 17.5 \text{ cm}^2$$

Then plug 17.5 into our volume formula:

$$V = Bh$$
$$V = (17.5)(12)$$
$$V = 210 \text{ cm}^3$$

Figure number 2 is a cylinder.

$$V = \pi r^2 h$$
$$V = (3.14)(6)^2(7)$$
$$V = (3.14)(36)(7)$$
$$V = 791.28 \text{ ft}^3$$

Figure number 3 is a pyramid. First we calculate the area of the base, which is a rectangle.

$$A = lw$$
$$A = (9)(12)$$
$$A = 108 \text{ in}^2$$

Then use 108 in our volume formula.

$$V = \left(\frac{1}{3}\right)Bh$$

$$V = \left(\frac{1}{3}\right)(108)(6.5)$$
$$V = 234 \text{ in}^3$$

Questions

Find the measure of the indicated angles.

1.

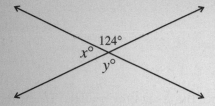

2.

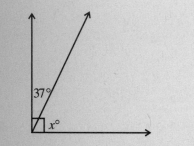

3.

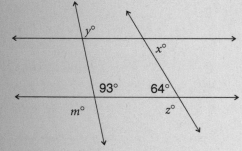

4. Two angles are supplementary. One angle measures 30 degrees less than three times the other. What are the measures of the angles?

Find the areas of the following triangles:

5.

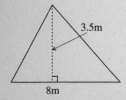

6.

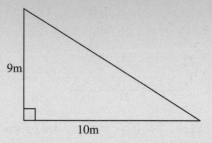

Find the missing angle measurements of the following triangles:

7.

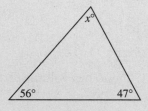

8.

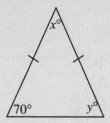

9. The ratio of the measures of the angles of a triangle is 3:4:5. What are the measures of the angles?

10. A ladder 13 ft long is placed against a side of a building with its bottom 5 ft away from the building. How high does the ladder reach up the side?

Find the areas of the following figures. Note that lines that appear to be parallel are, in fact, parallel, and angles that appear to be right are, in fact, right.

11.

12.

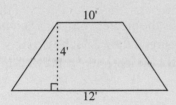

13.

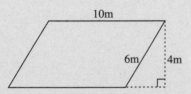

14.

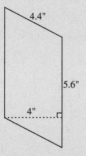

15. The length of a rectangle is 4 feet less than twice the width. If the perimeter is 52 m, then what are the dimensions of the rectangle?

Note: let $\pi = 3.14$ for all problems unless stated otherwise.

16. Find the area and circumference of a circle whose radius is 7 cm.

Find the area of the shaded regions. Let $\pi = 3.14$.

17.

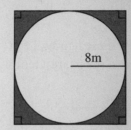

18.

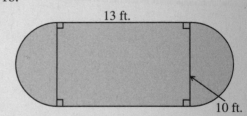

19. If the radius of a circle is doubled, what are the ratios of the circumference and area of the new circle to those of the original one?

20. A tire with a radius of 18 in. is rolled a total of 100 ft. How many complete revolutions does the tire make?

21.

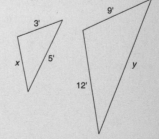

22. A 6 ft man casts a shadow 5 feet long. A flag-pole casts a shadow 35 feet long. How tall is the flagpole?

23. A map shows a drawing of a rectangular piece of ground, 5 mm by 14 mm. If the real width of the property is 333 m, then what is the real length?

Find the volume of these figures. Let $\pi = 3.14$. Round all answers to the nearest tenth.

24.

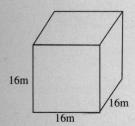

16m

16m

16m

25.

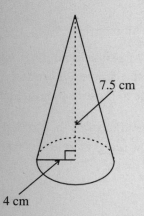

7.5 cm

4 cm

26.

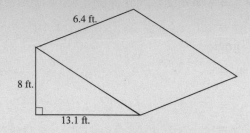

6.4 ft.

8 ft.

13.1 ft.

27. Which has the greater volume: a suitcase that measures 2 ft by 2.5 ft by .75 ft, or one that has the dimensions 1.5 ft by 2.3 ft by 1.2 ft?

Answers

1. $y = 124$ (vertical angles)

   $x = 180 - 124 = 56$ (supplementary angles)

2. $x = 90 - 37 = 53$ (complementary angles)

3. $x = 64$ (alternate interior angles)

   $y = 93$ (corresponding angles)

   $z = 180 - 64 = 116$ (supplementary angles)

   $m = 93$ (vertical angles)

4. Let $x =$ the smaller angle

   then $3x - 30 =$ the larger angle

   $x + 3x - 30 = 180$ (since angles are supplementary, their sum will be $180°$)

   $4x - 30 = 180$

   $4x = 210$

   $x = 52.5$

   The angles are $52.50°$ and $3(52.5) - 30 = 127.5°$

5. $A = \left(\dfrac{1}{2}\right)bh$

   $A = \left(\dfrac{1}{2}\right)(8)(3.5)$

   $A = 14 \text{ m}^2$

6. $A = \left(\dfrac{1}{2}\right)bh$

   $A = \left(\dfrac{1}{2}\right)(10)(9)$ (in a right triangle the legs

   can be used as the base and height of the figure)

   $A = 45 \text{ m}^2$

7. $x = 180 - (56 + 47)$ (since all 3 angles of a triangle sum to $180°$, we can subtract the two we know from 180 to find the third.

   $x = 180 - (103)$

   $x = 77$

   The missing angle is $77°$.

8. Since the base angles of an isosceles triangle are equal, the sum of the two base angles is $70° + 70° = 140°$. Subtracting this from $180°$ gives: $180° - 140° = 40°$.

9. $3x + 4x + 5x = 180$

   $12x = 180$

   $x = 15$

   $3(15°) = 45°$

   $4(15°) = 60°$

   $5(15°) = 75°$

10. $c^2 = a^2 + b^2$

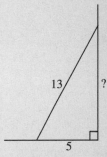

   $13^2 = 5^2 + b^2$

   $169 = 25 + b^2$

   $144 = b^2$

   $12 = b$

   The ladder reaches 12 ft up the wall.

11. $A = s^2$

 $A = 1.7^2$

 $A = 2.89 \text{ m}^2$

12. $A = \left(\dfrac{1}{2}\right)(b_1 + b_2)h$

 $A = \left(\dfrac{1}{2}\right)(10 + 12)(4)$

 $A = \left(\dfrac{1}{2}\right)(22)(4)$

 $A = 44 \text{ ft}^2$

13. $A = bh$

 $A = (10)(4)$

 $A = 40 \text{ m}^2$

14. $A = bh$

 $A = (4)(5.6)$

 $A = 22.4 \text{ in}^2$

15. Let w = width

 then $2w - 4$ = the length

 $P = 2l + 2w$

 $52 = 2(2w - 4) + 2(w)$

 $52 = 4w - 8 + 2w$

 $52 = 6w - 8$

 $60 = 6w$

 $10 = w$

 The width is 10 ft and the length is
 $2(10) - 4 = 16$ ft.

16. $A = \pi r^2 \qquad C = 2\pi r$

 $A = (3.14)(7)^2 \qquad C = 2(3.14)(7)$

 $A = (3.14)(49) \qquad C = 43.96 \text{ cm}$

 $A = 153.86 \text{ cm}^2$

17. Area of the shaded region = Area of the
 square − area of the circle

 $A = s^2 - \pi r^2$

 $A = 16^2 - (3.14)(8)^2$

 $A = 256 - (3.14)(64)$

 $A = 256 - 200.96$

 $A = 55.04 \text{ m}^2$

18. The two semicircles at either end can be
 thought of as combining to form an entire
 circle with radius 5, so

 Area of figure = Area of rectangle +
 area of circle

 $A = lw + \pi r^2$

 $A = (13)(10) + (3.14)(5)^2$

 $A = 130 + (3.14)(25)$

 $A = 130 + 78.5$

 $A = 208.5 \text{ ft}^2$

19. Let x = the radius of one circle.

 Then $2x$ will equal the radius of the other
 circle.

Comparing circumferences		Comparing the areas	
$C = 2\pi r$	$C = 2\pi r$	$A = r^2$	$A = \pi r^2$
$C = 2\pi(x)$	$C = 2\pi(2x)$	$A = \pi(x)^2$	$A = \pi(2x)^2$
$C = 2\pi x$	$C = 4\pi x$	$A = \pi x^2$	$A = 4\pi x^2$

 The circumference doubles.   The area quadruples.

20. First we have to convert to a common unit of measurement. You can convert 100 ft into 1200 in., or 18 in. to 1.5 ft.

    The circumference of the wheel is
    $C = 2(3.14)(1.5) = 9.42$ ft.
    If each revolution of the tire is 9.42 ft, then

    $\dfrac{100}{9.42} \approx 10.6.$

    Therefore, the tire will make 10 complete revolutions.

21. The ratio of two similar sides is 3:9 which can be reduced to 1:3.

    $\dfrac{1}{3} = \dfrac{5}{y}$ $\qquad$ $\dfrac{1}{3} = \dfrac{x}{12}$

    $y = 15$ ft $\qquad$ $3x = 12$

    $\qquad\qquad\quad$ $x = 4$ ft

22. $\dfrac{6}{5} = \dfrac{x}{35}$

    $210 = 5x$

    $42 = x$

    The flagpole is 42 ft high.

23. $\dfrac{5}{14} = \dfrac{333}{x}$

    $5x = 4662$

    $x = 932.4$

    The length is 932.4 m.

24. First find the area of the base (the square).

    $B = 16^2$

    $B = 256$ in^2

    Now put that into the volume formula:

    $V = Bh$

    $V = (256)(16)$

    $V = 4096$ m^3

25. The base of the cone is:

    $A = \pi r^2$

    $A = (3.14)(4)^2$

    $A = (3.14)(16)$

    $A = 50.24$ cm^2

    Now insert into the formula for a cone:

    $V = \dfrac{1}{3}Bh$

    $V = \dfrac{1}{3}(50.24)(7.5)$

    $V = 125.6$ cm^3

26. Area of the base:

    $A = \dfrac{1}{2}bh$

    $A = \dfrac{1}{2}(13.1)(8)$

    $\qquad A = 52.4$ ft^2

    $V = bh$

    $V = (52.4)(6.4)$

    $V = 335.36$ ft^3

27. Suitcase number 1 $= (2)(2.5)(.75) = 3.75$ ft^3

    Suitcase number 2 $= (1.5)(2.3)(1.2) = 4.14$ ft^3

    Suitcase number 2 will hold more.

Chapter 5

Analytic Geometry

A. Rectangular coordinates and definitions

Analytic geometry deals in part with graphing equations and inequalities on the coordinate plane. The rectangular coordinate plane consists of two number lines, called axes, that are placed perpendicular to each other. The "x-axis" is the horizontal number line and the "y-axis" is the vertical number line.

We can use the coordinate plane to graph equations containing two variables.

The two axes divide the plane into four regions. We call each of these regions *quadrants*, and designate them with roman numerals. The upper right-hand quadrant is called quadrant I; the other quadrants are numbered sequentially in a counter-clockwise direction. Any point on an axis is considered to not be in a quadrant.

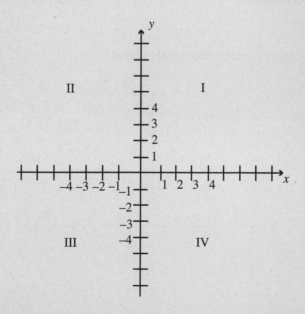

Any point on the plane can now be designated by a pair of numbers. The first number tells us how far to travel left or right on the x-axis, and the second number tells us how far to move up or down on the y-axis. We put both numbers in parentheses and call this point an *ordered pair*. Here are some ordered pairs and their locations in the rectangular coordinates:

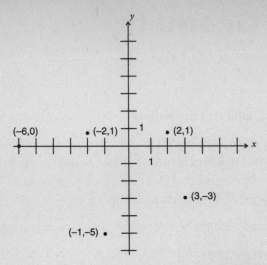

The point where the number lines cross has coordinates (0,0) and is called the origin.

The *x*-coordinate of an ordered pair is sometimes called the abscissa and the *y*-coordinate is called the ordinate.

Examples:

1. Name these points on the coordinate plane:

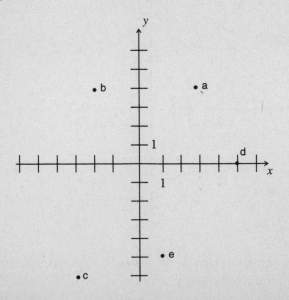

a.   is (3, 4) since it 3 units to the right and 4 units up

b.   is (−2, 4), since it is 2 units to the left and 4 units up

c.   is (−3, −6) since it is 3 units to the left and 6 units down

d.   is (5, 0) since it is 5 units to the right on the x-axis

e.   is (1, −5) since it is 1 unit to the right and 5 units down

2.   Graph these points on the coordinate plane:

a.   (2, 2)

b.   (−3, 0)

c.   (−1, −3)

d.   (−3, −1)

e.   (0, −5)

f.   (3, −3)

As we did in the previous example, for each point, start from the origin and move horizontally, based on the x-coordinate. Then move vertically, based on the y-coordinate, and then make a dot showing the point you graphed. The letters of the problem are included here to make sure that you have plotted the correct coordinate in the correct locations.

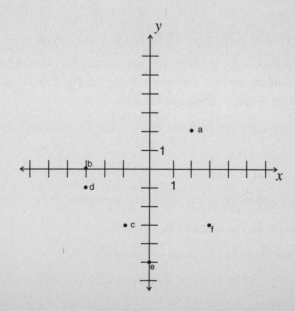

B. Slope

Slope is a number that can be assigned to any straight line that is graphed on the coordinate plane. It is a measure of how "steep" the line is. It is standard to let the variable *m* stand for slope. By convention, a line that ascends from left to right has a positive slope, and a line that descends from left to right has a negative slope. A horizontal line has a slope of 0, since it has no "slant." A vertical line has no slope (or an undefined or infinite slope).

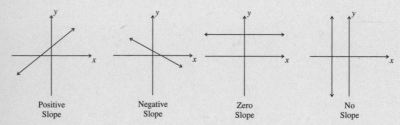

| Positive | Negative | Zero | No |
| Slope | Slope | Slope | Slope |

One way to calculate the exact value of the slope of a line is to find any two points that are on the line and use the formula $m = \frac{y_2 - y_1}{x_2 - x_1}$. In this formula, (x_1, y_1) and (x_2, y_2) represent the coordinates of the two points that are being used. It makes no difference to the final answer which ordered pair—(x_1, y_1) or (x_2, y_2)—you let stand for which point. Sometimes this formula is rewritten using the Greek letter Δ (delta), as $m = \frac{\Delta y}{\Delta x}$.

The slope can be used to help graph a line. If a line has a slope of $\frac{2}{3}$, for example, we know that as the *y*-value changes 2, the *x*-value changes 3. So to graph the line, locate one point on the line, move 3 units to the right and 2 units up and make another mark on the graph to trace out the line.

Thus, once you have the slope and any one point, you can easily draw the graph of the right line.

Examples:

1. Calculate the slope of the given pairs of coordinates:

    a. (2, 3) and (3, 2) The slope of this line is -1.

    b. $(-2, -5)$ and (4, 5) The slope of this line is $\frac{5}{3}$.

    c. (4, 1) and (6, 1) The slope of this line is 0, thus the line is horizontal.

2. Draw a graph of the straight line containing the point (2,3) with a slope of 3. Write the slope of 3 as $\frac{3}{1}$. From the point (2, 3), move 3 units up and 1 unit to the and make another mark.

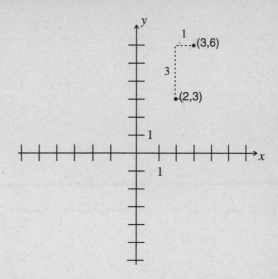

If desired, we can start from this new coordinate, (3, 6), and again move 3 up and 1 right to make another mark:

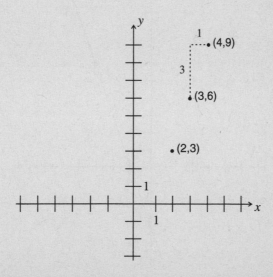

Since $\frac{3}{1}$ has the same value as $\frac{3}{-1}$, we also could have moved down 3 units (negative 3) and to the left 1 and made a mark:

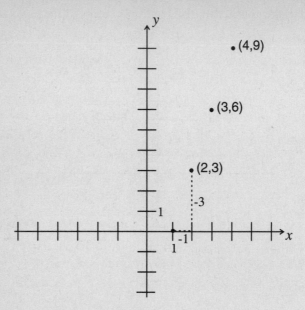

Connecting the dots gives the graph of the line:

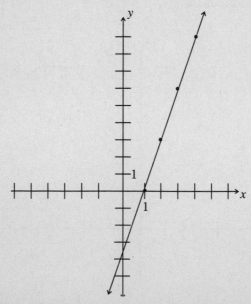

Note that it was really necessary to find only one point in addition to (2, 3) to graph the line.

C. Graphing straight lines

An equation in two variables, where both variables are to the first power, will always have a straight line as its graph. One way to graph this straight line is to use the *table method*. In this method, you make a list of ordered pairs that satisfy the equation and graph them.

A quicker and surer method is to rewrite the equation so that the variable y is on one side of the equation and everything else is on the other. This is called the *slope-intercept* form of an equation, and we say that you have put the equation into the form $y = mx + b$, where m stands for the slope and b stands for the y-intercept, which is the y-coordinate of the point where the line crosses the y-axis. Start drawing your graph by marking a point at b on the y-axis, then use the slope m to move to the next point on your graph.

The examples below will show both methods for graphing lines, but the solutions to the exercises will only show the slope-intercept method.

If the equation of the line only contains one variable, then the graph will be either a vertical or horizontal line. An equation in the form $y = k$, where k is any number, is a horizontal line passing through the y-axis at k. An equation of the form $x = h$, where h is any number, is a vertical line passing through the x-axis at h.

Examples:

Graph the following lines:

1. $x + 3y = -3$

   Using the table method, we must find values for x and y that will make the equation true. This can be done mentally, or by picking a number for x or y and then substituting it into the equation in order to find the corresponding coordinate.

x	y
0	-1
3	-2
-3	0

   You should use at least 3 points to help avoid errors. Thus, graphing these three coordinates will give us the graph of the line $x + 3y = -3$. Note that you may come up with 3 totally different points using the table method, but your line will look the same.

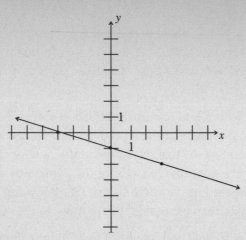

We can also solve this equation by rewriting the equation in the slope-intercept form.

$x + 3y = -3$

$3y = -x - 3$ (subtracting x from both sides)

$y = (-\frac{1}{3})x - 1$ (dividing all terms by 3)

Now we see that the y-intercept is at $(0, -1)$ and the slope is $-\frac{1}{3}$.

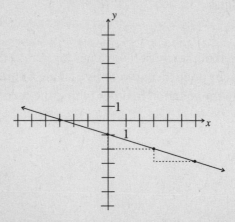

2. $y = -2x - 1$

Using the table method we find three points that solve the equation.

x	y
0	-1
2	-5
-1	1

Graphing these points on the coordinate plane gives us the straight line graph.

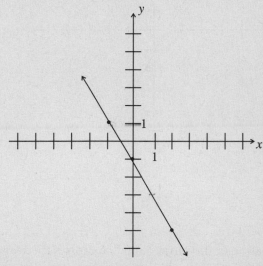

Now, note that the given equation is already in slope intercept form. Mark a point at $(0, -1)$ since the value of the y-intercept, b, is -1. Since the slope m is -2, which can be thought of as $\dfrac{-2}{1}$, we move two units down the y-axis (since the slope is a negative number) from b and then 1 unit to the right on the x-axis. Repeating the process gives us the points we need to draw the graph.

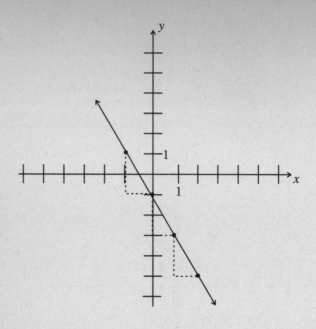

3. $x = 4$

    $x = 4$ is the equation of the vertical line that crosses the x-axis at $(4, 0)$.

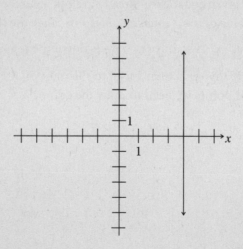

4. $y = -3$

$y = -3$ is the equation for the horizontal line that crosses the $y-$axis at $(0, -3)$.

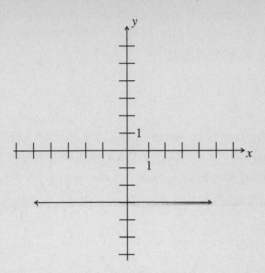

Some of the questions that follow ask you to graph two equations on one set of axis and find the point of intersection. There are three possible outcomes: the lines meet at one point, they are parallel (and thus don't intersect at all), or they are really the same line (called coincident lines).

D. Graphing inequalities

The graph of a straight line divides the coordinate plane into 3 regions. The line itself is where all ordered pairs that solve the equation are located. On one side of this line are all ordered pairs for which the left side of the equation actually has a larger value than the right side. The other side of the line contains all ordered pairs for which the left side of the equation actually has a smaller value than the right side. Knowing this, when we graph an inequality we will shade in one side of the line showing where all the ordered pairs that make the statement true are located.

Graphing an inequality begins the same way as graphing a straight line. Rewrite the inequality as $y > mx + b$, $y < mx + b$, $y \geq mx + b$, or $y \leq mx + b$. Then, locate some points so that you can draw the graph of $y = mx + b$.

If the inequality is > or <, then the line itself does not get drawn in. Instead, a dotted line is drawn to show that the ordered pairs that solve the equation are not included in

97

the solution. If the inequality is ≤ or ≥, then the line drawn is solid. In either case, after the line is indicated, one of the sides will be shaded in.

Just as the graphs of simultaneous equations allow you to find the point of intersection, the graphs of simultaneous inequalities allow you to find the area of intersection, i.e., where the shading overlaps. Also, as with simultaneous equations, there is the possibility that there is no overlap at all.

Examples:

Graph $y - 2x < 5$

First, we add $2x$ to both sides to put the inequality into the form $y < mx + b$. Thus, the new form of the inequality is $y < 2x + 5$. On a piece of graph paper we draw a point at $(0, 5)$ and start using a slope of $\frac{2}{1}$ to draw other points on the graph. Since the inequality symbol is $<$ and not $\leq$, a dotted line is drawn as follows:

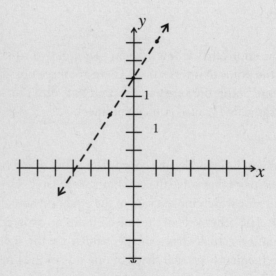

To determine which side of the line should be shaded, pick any point which is not on the line and substitute it into the inequality. If the point you chose solves the inequality, then that point, as well as every other point on that side of the line, makes the inequality true and therefore that is the side of the line to shade in. On the other hand, if the point you chose made the inequality false, then no point on that side makes the inequality true. Thus, only points on the other side of the line make the inequality a true one and are shaded in. In the example above, the point $(0, 0)$ is not on the line, so we substitute it into the inequality.

$y - 2x < 5$

$0 - 2(0) < 5$

$0 - 0 < 5$

$0 < 5$

$0 < 5$ is a true statement, so all the points on the side of the line that includes $(0, 0)$ are shaded in.

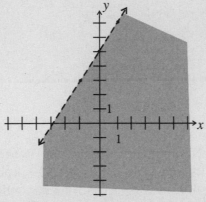

Graph $y \geq x - 3$.

Since the inequality symbol is $\geq$, the line drawn will be a solid line. Starting at $(0, -3)$ and noting that the slope is 1 enables us to find the graph of the line.

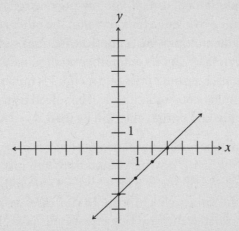

Picking the point $(0, 0)$ and substituting it into the inequality, we come up with the inequality $0 > -3$. Since this is true, every point on the side of the line which contains $(0, 0)$ must be shaded.

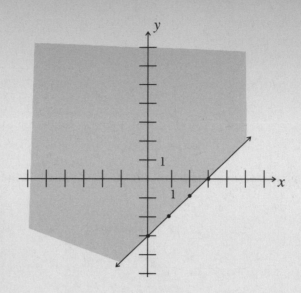

E. Simultaneous equations

We have already graphed simultaneous equations (exercises 25–30). Graphing is one way to determine where two lines intersect. The problem with this method is that it is often difficult to read the exact coordinates of the point of intersection off of the graph.

There are two easy methods to solve simultaneous equations algebraically. In one method, called the *substitution method*, you rewrite one equation in the form $y = \ldots$ or $x = \ldots$ and substitute that value for x or y into the other equation. In the *addition-subtraction method*, you multiply one (or both) equations so that upon adding them together one of the variables cancels out. Either method may be used for any set of simultaneous equations, but sometimes one method is much easier than the other. In the examples, the simultaneous equations will be solved using both methods. In the exercises, either one method or the other will be used.

Sometimes when working with simultaneous equations, as you try to cancel out one variable both will cancel, leaving an equation with just numbers. If that resulting equation is a true one (like $4 = 4$ or $-3 = -3$), then the equations you were working with were the same to begin with. In this case, we say that "all solutions" work. If, on the other hand, the resulting equation is false (like $3 = -5$ or $2 = 1$), then the two lines are parallel and there is no point of intersection. We say that "no solutions" work.

Examples:

Solve these simultaneous equations.

$$y = 17 - x$$
$$x - y = 3$$

To use the substitution method, note that the first equation is already written as $y = 17 - x$. Substituting $17 - x$ in the second equation for y gives us:

$$x - (17 - x) = 3$$
$$x - 17 + x = 3$$
$$2x - 17 = 3$$
$$2x = 20$$
$$x = 10$$

So the x-coordinate is 10. Take this number and substitute it into either equation to solve for the y-coordinate.

$$y = 17 - x$$
$$y = 17 - 10$$
$$y = 7$$

So, the ordered pair $(10, 7)$ is the point of intersection of the two lines.

To solve the same problem using the addition method, we must rewrite the equations so that there are corresponding terms on both sides of the equal sign. For example, we can rewrite the first equation as $x + y = 17$. Now the equations can be lined up.

$$x + y = 17$$
$$x - y = 3$$

Now, by adding both sides of the equations together (just like in a regular addition problem), we get:

$$x + y = 17$$
$$\underline{x - y = 3}$$
$$2x = 20 \ (x + x = 2x, y - y = 0, \text{ and } 17 + 3 = 20)$$

Solving for x:

$$2x = 20$$
$$x = 10$$

So $x = 10$ is the solution. Substituting back into either equation gives the value for the other variable.

$x + y = 17$

$10 + y = 17$

$y = 7$

The solution is $(10, 7)$.

Solve the system of equations:

$x + 3y = 26$

$3x + 2y = 29$

Using the substitution method, we solve the first equation for x, obtaining $x = -3y + 26$. Substituting into the second equation:

$3x + 2y = 29$

$3(-3y + 26) + 2y = 29$

$-9y + 78 + 2y = 29$

$-7y + 78 = 29$

$-7y = -49$

$y = 7$

Substituting 7 for y into the first equation:

$x + 3y = 26$

$x + 3(7) = 26$

$x + 21 = 26$

$x = 5$

The solution is $(5, 7)$.

Using the addition-subtraction method, note that neither variable will cancel if we add the two equations together as is. In such a case, we must multiply one or both of the equations by a number so that either the x or y terms will cancel out when we add them. For example, if we multiply the first equation by -3, we get:

$$-3(x + 3y = 26) \qquad -3x - 9y = -78 \quad \leftarrow \text{multiplying the first}$$

equation by -3

$$3x + 2y = 29 \qquad \underline{3x + 2y = 29} \quad \leftarrow \text{copying down the}$$

second equation

$$-7y = -49 \quad \leftarrow \text{adding the equations together}$$

$$y = 7$$

Substituting into either equation, as before, gives the solution for x.

Multiplying the first equation by -3 is not the only way to solve this system of equations. If we had multiplied the top equation by 2 and the bottom equation by -3, for example, then we would have a $6y$ and a $-6y$ to cancel.

F. Finding areas

You should be able to graph a geometric figure on graph paper and then determine the area of the figure. If the shape you have graphed is one for which you don't have an area formula, then you should be able to divide the figure into smaller regions for which you know the area formulas, and then add those results together.

Some area formulas you should know are:

Square $A = s^2$, where s is the length of a side

Rectangle $A = lw$ (length times width)

Triangle $A = \frac{1}{2}bh$ (one-half base times height)

Parallelogram $A = bh$ (base times height)

Trapezoid $A = \frac{1}{2}(b_1 + b_2)h$ (b_1 and b_2 are the two different bases)

Examples:

The coordinates $(4, 2)$, $(11, 2)$, $(9, 5)$, and $(5, 5)$ form a trapezoid. What is the area of the figure?

Drawing a diagram helps us visualize the figure.

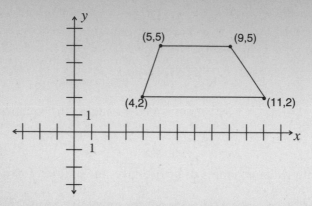

The two bases are the two parallel sides. By counting, we can see that the lengths of the bases are 7 and 4 units. The height can be seen to be 3 units. Using the formula for the area of a trapezoid we can find the answer.

$$A = \left(\frac{1}{2}\right)(b_1 + b_2)h$$

$$A = \left(\frac{1}{2}\right)(7 + 4)(3)$$

$$A = \left(\frac{1}{2}\right)(11)(3)$$

$$A = 16.5 \text{ square units}$$

Find the area of figure $ABCDE$ with vertices $A(1, 1)$, $B(1, 5)$, $C(4, 7)$, $D(6, 5)$, and $E(6, 1)$.

Again, a diagram helps us to visualize the figure and determine how to find the area.

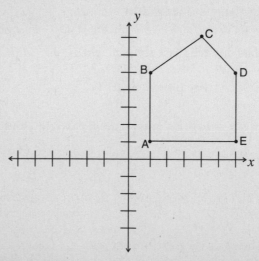

Since there is no simple formula for this figure, the method of solving involves dividing this figure up into smaller figures and then finding the area of each one. In this case, the figure can be divided into a rectangle $ABDE$ and a triangle BCD.

$$\text{Area of } ABCDE = \text{Area } BCD + \text{Area } ABDE$$

$$= \left(\frac{1}{2}\right)(5)(2) + (5)(4)$$

$$= 5 + 20$$

$$= 25 \text{ square units}$$

G. Direct variation

To say that two quantities vary directly (or are in direct variation to each other) is to say that as one quantity increases, the other will increase as well. They do not necessarily increase by the same amount, but they do increase in proportion to each other.

In general, to say that two variables x and y are in direct variation is to say that they can be related by the equation $y = kx$, where k is some constant, called the constant of variation. Given a fact about two variables that are in direct variation with each other, we can find the value of the constant k and use it to solve other questions about the relationship.

Examples:

If y is directly proportional to x and $x = 8$ when $y = 14$, then what is the value of y when x is 12?

Since y is directly proportional to x, the formula $y = kx$ is used. We are given that when x is 8, y is 14. Using this fact, we can find the value of the constant of variation, k.

$$y = kx$$

$$14 = k(8)$$

$$14 = 8k$$

$$1.75 = k$$

Now we have the value of the constant of variation and can use the new equation $y = 1.75x$ to find the answer to the question.

$$y = 1.75x$$

$$y = 1.75(12)$$

$$y = 21$$

The number of bushels of grain a farm produces is in direct variation with the number of acres planted. If 25 acres produce 3,000 bushels, then:

a.   How many bushels will 35 acres produce?

b.   How many acres are needed to produce 10,000 bushels?

First we define our variables. Let's let x = the number of acres used and y = the number of bushels produced. Then we can use the equation $y = kx$ and substitute our known fact (25 acres produce 3,000 bushels) to find the constant of variation:

$y = kx$

$3{,}000 = k(25)$

$3{,}000 = 25k$

$120 = k$

Knowing the constant of variation, we now have an equation $y = 120x$, which we can use to answer both parts a and b.

a. $y = 120x$

$y = 120(35)$

$y = 4{,}200$ bushels

b. $y = 120x$

$10{,}000 = 120x$

$x = 83\frac{1}{3}$ acres are needed.

Questions

1. Plot these points on the coordinate axis and tell what quadrant they are in.

   a. $(2, 3)$
   b. $(-4, 0)$
   c. $(1, -1)$
   d. $(-5, 4)$
   e. $(0, 0)$
   f. $(-2, -5)$

Find the slope of a line through the given coordinates.

2. $(3, 3)$ and $(6, 6)$

3. $(3, 1)$ and $(-4, 0)$

4. $(2, 6)$ and $(-2, 6)$

5. $(-.5, 3.5)$ and $(2.5, 7.5)$

6. $(-3, -3)$ and $(-2, -6)$

7. $(1, -1)$ and $(-2, 2)$

Draw a graph of the straight line that contains the following point and has the indicated slope:

8. point $(3, 4)$ and slope $\frac{1}{3}$

Graph the following:

9. $y = \left(\frac{-1}{3}\right)x - 2$

Graph each set of two equations on the same axes graph and find the point of intersection.

10. $5x + 2y = 4$
    $2x - y = 7$

11. $3x = 2y - 6$
    $6 = 6y - 9x$

Graph the following inequalities.

12. $y < 2x$

13. $2x < 6y - 12$

Solve these systems of equations by using either the substitution or addition-subtraction method.

14. $2x + y = 11$
    $2x - y = 9$

15. $3x - y = 10$
    $y = 2x - 40$

16. $x - y = 26$
    $3x - 8y = 3$

17. $x + y = 37$
    $x = 12 - y$

18. The coordinates of a triangle are $A(2, 3)$, $B(2, 10)$, and $C(-3, 3)$. Find the area of the triangle.

19. Find the area of the figure $ABCD$ with $A(-9, 2)$, $B(-6, 5)$, $C(-3, 2)$, and $D(-6, -2)$.

20. y is directly proportional to x and x is 18 when y is 8. What is x when y is 6?

21. The elongation of a spring is directly propor-
    tional to the weight attached to it. If 15g
    stretches a spring 5 cm, then what weight will
    stretch the spring 12 cm? How far will the
    spring stretch with a weight of 22g attached?

22. In a circuit of 48 volts, a voltmeter
    registers 60. The voltmeter's scale only
    goes up to 100. What is the maximum
    number of volts the voltmeter can
    measure?

Answers

1.

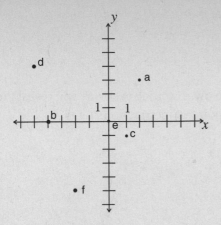

a is in Quadrant I, d is in quadrant II, c is in quadrant IV, and f is in quadrant III. b and e are on an axis and are therefore not in a quadrant.

2. Use the formula $m = \frac{y_2 - y_1}{x_2 - x_1}$ for calculating slope:

$$m = \frac{6 - 3}{6 - 3}$$

$$m = \frac{3}{3}$$

$$m = 1$$

The slope of the line is 1.

3. Use the formula $m = \frac{y_2 - y_1}{x_2 - x_1}$ for calculating slope:

$$m = \frac{0 - 1}{-4 - 3}$$

$$m = \frac{-1}{-7} \text{ or } \frac{1}{7}$$

4. Use the formula $m = \frac{y_2 - y_1}{x_2 - x_1}$ for calculating slope:

$$m = \frac{6 - 6}{-2 - 2}$$

$$m = \frac{0}{-4}$$

$$m = 0$$

Note that the slope is 0 (i.e., a horizontal line). If the zero had appeared in the denominator then there would be no slope (a vertical line) since you cannot divide by zero.

5. Use the formula $m = \frac{y_2 - y_1}{x_2 - x_1}$ for calculating slope:

$$m = \frac{7.5 - 3.5}{2.5 - (-.5)}$$

$$m = \frac{4}{3}$$

6. Use the formula $m = \frac{(y_2 - y_1)}{(x_2 - x_1)}$ for calculating slope:

$$m = \frac{-6 - (-3)}{-2 - (-3)}$$

$$m = \frac{-3}{1}$$

$$m = -3$$

7. Use the formula $m = \frac{y_2 - y_1}{x_2 - x_1}$ for calculating slope:

$$m = \frac{2 - (-1)}{-2 - 1}$$

$$m = \frac{3}{-3}$$

$$m = -1$$

8. Starting at the point (3, 4) on the graph paper, we can move either up 1 and to the right 3 or down 1 and to the left 3 (thinking of the slope of $\frac{1}{3}$ as $\frac{-1}{-3}$, which it is equivalent to).

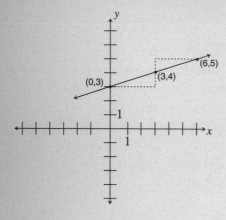

9. $y = \left(\dfrac{-1}{3}\right)x - 2$

    This line is already in $y = mx + b$ form. The slope is $\dfrac{-1}{3}$ and the y-intercept is $(0, -2)$. Plot the point $(0, -2)$ on the graph, and then count either one down and three to the right or 1 up and 3 to the to left plot other points on the graph.

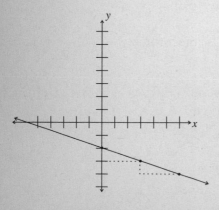

10. Putting both equations in slope intercept form gives us:

    $5x + 2y = 4$ $\qquad$ $2x - y = 7$
    $2y = -5x + 4$ $\qquad$ $-y = -2x + 7$
    $y = -\dfrac{5}{2}x + 2$ $\qquad$ $y = 2x - 7$

    Now, graphing each one will reveal the point of intersection:

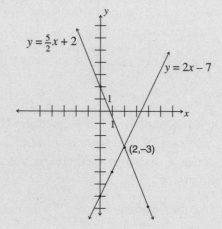

    So the point of intersection is $(2, -3)$.

11. $3x = 2y - 6$ $\qquad$ $6 = 6y - 9x$
    $2y - 6 = 3x$ $\qquad$ $6y - 9x = 6$
    $2y = 3x + 6$ $\qquad$ $6y = 9x + 6$
    $y = \left(\dfrac{3}{2}\right)x + 3$ $\qquad$ $y = \left(\dfrac{3}{2}\right)x + 1$

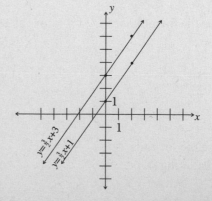

These lines are parallel and will have no point of intersection. You can also tell that these lines are parallel from their equal slopes.

12. To graph $y < 2x$, we begin by graphing $y = 2x$. This line has a slope of 2 and a y-intercept of 0. Since the inequality is $<$ and not $\leq$, the line drawn will be a dotted line and not a solid line. Let's pick the point $(5, 1)$ and substitute it into the inequality.

$y < 2x$
$1 < 2(5)$
$1 < 10$ which is true, so the side of the inequality containing $(5, 1)$ is the side that gets shaded in.

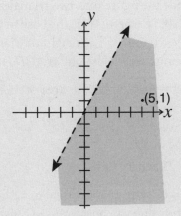

13. $2x < 6y - 12$

$6y - 12 > 2x$
$6y > 2x + 12$
$y > \left(\dfrac{1}{3}\right)x + 2$

Using the point $(0, 0)$:

$0 \geq \left(\dfrac{1}{3}\right)(0) + 2$
$0 \geq 2$ is false, so the side not containing $(0, 0)$ will be shaded.

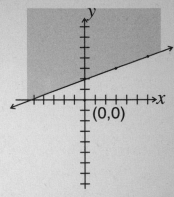

14. Since the equations contain a y and a $-y$ already, it is easiest to use the addition-subtraction method to solve.

$2x + y = 11$
$\underline{2x - y = 9}$
$4x = 20$
$x = 5$

Next substitute 5 for x in the first equation and solve for y.

$2(5) + y = 11$
$10 + y = 11$
$y = 1$
The solution is $(5, 1)$.

15. Since the second equation is already set up in the form $y = \ldots$, use the substitution method:

$3x - (2x - 40) = 10$
$3x - 2x + 40 = 10$
$x + 40 = 10$
$x = -30$

Substituting $x = -30$ into either equation (in this case, the second)

$y = 2(-30) - 40$
$y = -60 - 40$
$y = -100$
The solution is $(-30, -100)$.

16. Using the addition-subtraction method:

$x - y = 26$ (times -3) $\quad -3x + 3y = -78$
$3x - 8y = 3$
$$\underline{\quad 3x - 8y = 3 \quad}$$
$$-5y = -75$$
$$y \;\;\;\; = 15$$

$x - 15 = 26$
$x = 41$

The solution is (41, 15).

17. $x + y = 37$

$x = 12 - y$
$(12 - y) + y = 37$
$12 - y + y = 37$
$12 = 37$

The statement $12 = 37$ is false, so there is no solution to this problem. These lines, if graphed, would be parallel.

18. First draw a picture to visualize the figure.

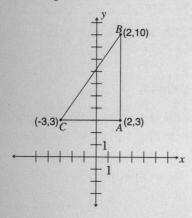

Use AC as the base (with a length of 5) and AB as our height (with a length of 7):

$A = \dfrac{1}{2} bh$

$A = \dfrac{1}{2}(5)(7)$

$A = \dfrac{1}{2}(35)$

$A = 17.5$ square units

19.

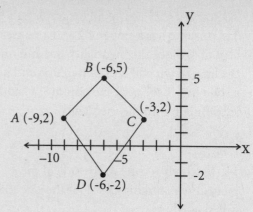

Divide the figure into two triangles ABC and ACD, where AC is the base of both triangles (6 units). The height of triangle ABC is 3 units and the height of ACD is 4 units.

Area = Area of ABC + area of ACD

$A = \left(\dfrac{1}{2}\right)(6)(3) + \left(\dfrac{1}{2}\right)(6)(4)$

$A = 9 + 12$
$A = 21$ square units

20. If y is directly proportional to x, then the relationship can be expressed as $y = kx$. Next, substitute to find the constant of variation using the fact that x is 18 when y is 8:

$y = kx$
$8 = k(18)$
$8 = 18k$
$\dfrac{4}{9} = k$

So $y = \left(\dfrac{4}{9}\right)x$.

When y is 6:

$6 = \dfrac{4}{9} x$

$13.5 = x$

21. Let e = elongation of the spring

Let w = weight

$e = kw$

$5 = k(15)$

$5 = 15k$

$\dfrac{1}{3} = k$

$e = \left(\dfrac{1}{3}\right)w$

$12 = \left(\dfrac{1}{3}\right)w$

$36 \text{ g} = w$

Next,

$e = \dfrac{1}{3} w$

$e = \dfrac{1}{3}(22)$

$e = \dfrac{22}{3}$ or $7\dfrac{1}{3}$ cm

22. Let v = volts

Let m = meter reading

$v = km$

$48 = k(60)$

$48 = 60k$

$\dfrac{4}{5} = k$

$v = \left(\dfrac{4}{5}\right)m$

$v = \left(\dfrac{4}{5}\right)(100)$

$v = 80$ volts

Chapter 6

Probability

A. Basic probability

The probability of some event occurring is defined by the fraction:

number of wanted outcomes
number of possible outcomes

To this fraction we assign the notation $P(E)$, where P stands for the phrase *the probability that*, and E is the event we want to find the probability of. For example, the probability of tossing a coin and having it land heads could be written $P(\text{head})$. To find this probability, note that there are exactly two possible outcomes of flipping a coin, heads or tails. Therefore the denominator of the fraction will be 2. There is only one "wanted" outcome, and this is getting heads on the toss. Thus we can write:

$$P(\text{heads}) = \frac{1}{2}$$

Examples:

1. What is the probability of rolling one die and getting an even number?

    A die has 6 possible outcomes (the numbers 1 through 6) and 3 of them (2, 4, and 6) are the wanted outcomes. Therefore $P(\text{even number}) = \frac{3}{6} = \frac{1}{2}$.

2. What is the probability of pulling one card out of a poker deck and having it be a club?

    There are 52 possible outcomes (since there are 52 cards in the deck). 13 of the cards are clubs, so $P(\text{club}) = \frac{13}{52} = \frac{1}{4}$.

B. *And* and probability

We will now see how to compute the probability that two events happen at the same time. If A and B are two events, the probability that they both happen at the same time can be written $P(A \text{ and } B)$.

Many such problems can be solved through a simple listing of the desired outcomes. If the listing of possibilities gets too complicated or cumbersome, or if the problem already gives you the probabilities for A and B, then there is a formula for *and* probability questions as well. The formula is $P(A \text{ and } B) = P(A) \, P(B \mid A)$. The second probability $(B \mid A)$ means the probability of B given that A has already occurred. The examples as well as the exercises will contain both methods of arriving at the answer whenever possible.

Examples:

1. A card is drawn from a poker deck. What is the probability that the card is black and a 6?

    There are 26 cards that are black, and there are 4 cards that are a 6. However, only the 6 of spades and the 6 of clubs fit the category of being both black and a 6. Therefore, $P(\text{black and } 6) = \dfrac{2}{52} = \dfrac{1}{26}$.

    Let A represent the event of drawing a black card, and B represent the event of drawing a 6. Then $P(A) = P(\text{BLACK})$, $P(B) = P(6)$, and $P(B \mid A) = P(6 \text{ given that the chosen card is black})$. We will use the formula $P(A \text{ and } B) = P(A) \, P(B \mid A)$.

    $P(\text{black}) = \dfrac{26}{52}$ or $\dfrac{1}{2}$. Given that we have now selected one of the 26 black cards, there are only 2 sixes in the group, namely the 6 of spades and the 6 of clubs. So $P(\text{a } 6 \mid \text{black}) = \dfrac{2}{26}$. Notice that the denominator is now 26, since it is given that we already have only the black cards to deal with. So:

    $$
    \begin{aligned}
    P(A \text{ and } B) \quad &= P(A) \, P(B \mid A) \\[6pt]
    &= \left(\frac{1}{2}\right)\left(\frac{2}{26}\right) \\[6pt]
    &= \left(\frac{1}{2}\right)\left(\frac{1}{13}\right) \\[6pt]
    &= \frac{1}{26}
    \end{aligned}
    $$

2. The numbers 1 through 10 are placed in a hat and one number is drawn at random. What is the probability that the number is odd and a prime number?

    The set of odd numbers is $\{1,3,5,7,9\}$ and the set of prime numbers is $\{2,3,5,7\}$. The overlapping set will be $\{3,5,7\}$. Then $P(\text{prime} \mid \text{odd}) = \dfrac{3}{10}$. Again, using the formula, let A be the event that the number is odd and let B be the event that it is a prime. There are 5 odd numbers, so $P(\text{odd}) = \dfrac{5}{10}$ or $\dfrac{1}{2}$. The $P(\text{prime} \mid \text{odd}) = \dfrac{3}{5}$, since three of the 5 odd numbers are prime. So:

    $$P(A \text{ and } B) \qquad = P(A)\,P(B \mid A)$$

    $$= \left(\frac{1}{2}\right)\left(\frac{3}{5}\right)$$

    $$= \frac{3}{10}$$

C. *Or* and probability

    In this section, we will see how to compute the probability that either event A or event B occurs.

    The formula for computing such probabilities is $P(A \text{ or } B) = P(A) + P(B) - P(A \text{ and } B)$. Simply stated, this formula says that in order to find the probability of either of two events occurring, take the separate probabilities of the two events, add them together, and then subtract the probability that both events happen.

    As before in the *and* problems, the quickest way to find such probabilities is to try to list the possibilities instead of using the formula. However, sometimes that is difficult to do. In the examples and exercises here, we will use the formula every time, but remember that some problems can also be done by listing.

    Examples:

    1. In a deck of 52 cards, one is chosen at random. What is the probability that the card is red or a jack?

        There are 26 red cards, so $P(\text{red}) = \dfrac{26}{52}$

        There are 4 jacks, so $P(\text{jack}) = \dfrac{4}{52}$

But there is an overlap here. Two cards, namely the jack of hearts and the jack of diamonds, are being counted twice. These two items have been counted in both categories above. Therefore, the probability that a red jack is selected must be subtracted from your answer.

So, $P(\text{red or jack})$ $= P(\text{red}) + P(\text{jack}) - P(\text{red and jack})$

$$= \frac{26}{52} + \frac{4}{52} - \frac{2}{52}$$

$$= \frac{28}{52} \text{ or } \frac{7}{13}$$

2. What is the probability of drawing a red seven or a black face card from a deck of 52 cards?

There are 2 red sevens, so $P(\text{red 7}) = \frac{2}{52}$.

There are 6 black face cards, so $P(\text{black face card}) = \frac{6}{52}$.

In this case, there is no overlap, so the probabilities can simply be added together for the final answer: $\frac{2}{52} + \frac{6}{52} = \frac{8}{52} \text{ or } \frac{2}{13}$.

D. Complements

If the probability of rain today is 20 percent, then what is the probability of it not raining?

The word *not* is described in probability as the complement of the probability. By definition, the $P(\text{not } A) = 1 - P(A)$. This makes intuitive sense since the probability of an event not happening added to the probability of an event happening should be 1. To answer the above question then, the $P(\text{not raining}) = 1 - P(\text{raining}) = 1 - .20 = .80$. There is an 80 percent chance of it not raining tomorrow.

Examples:

1. What is the probability of not drawing a face card out of a deck of 52 poker cards?

This is easy to figure out using complements. The probability of getting a face card is $\frac{12}{52}$, (4 jacks, 4 queens, and 4 kings). Using our definition of complement:

$$P(\text{not face card}) = 1 - P(\text{face card})$$

$$= 1 - \frac{12}{52}$$

$$= \frac{40}{52} \text{ or } \frac{10}{13}$$

2. What is the probability that a number chosen from the numbers 1 through 20 is not a prime number?

    The number of primes between 1 and 20 is 8 (2, 3, 5, 7, 11, 13, 17, and 19), so:

    $$P(\text{not a prime}) = 1 - P(\text{prime}) = 1 - \frac{8}{20} = \frac{12}{20} = \frac{3}{5}$$

E. Tree Diagrams

Besides simply listing the desired events as we have thus far, there are several other ways we can think about the number of events in a probability problem. These techniques will make it easier to count the total number of ways that an event can occur (the denominator of our probability problem) as well as to help us find the number of favorable ways the event occurs (the numerator of our problem). The next few sections concentrate on the counting of events.

One of the methods of counting is called a *tree diagram*. From a starting point, arrows come out indicating the possibilities of the first step or choice. For example, let's start flipping a coin. If a coin is flipped once, then the tree diagram would look like this:

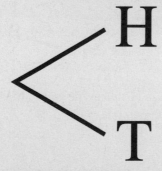

Here, H stands for heads and T for tails. As you can see, there are two possible outcomes when flipping a coin once. If the coin is flipped again, from each previous H or

T more branches arise. Notice the second flip is indicated twice since each of the original branches of the tree needs to have the second flip associated with it.

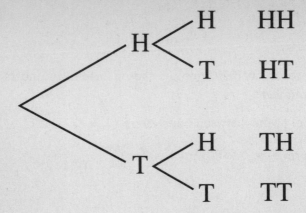

There are four distinct possibilities after two flips: HH, HT, TH, and TT. Suppose the coin was flipped a third time:

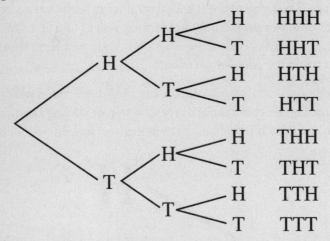

Now there are 8 possibilities, all listed at the end of the tree diagram. This list of all possible outcomes is called the *sample space*.

Examples:

1, Create a tree diagram to show the sample space for the following scenarios:

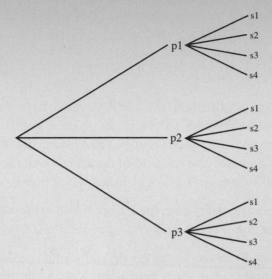

a. If you have 3 pairs of pants and four shirts, how many different outfits can you make out of the various combinations?

A tree diagram showing the 3 pairs of pants (p1, p2, and p3) as well as the four shirts (s1, s2, s3, and s4) is shown above. Note that it does not matter whether the pants or shirts are used first in the tree diagram; the sample space will still be the same.

As the tree diagram shows, there are 12 different outfits that can be worn using different combinations of shirts and pants.

b. A coin is flipped 3 times. What is the probability of getting exactly 2 heads in the 3 tosses?

Here is the tree diagram we developed earlier.

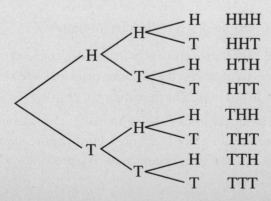

Analyzing the sample space, we see 3 events that contain two heads (HHT, HTH, and THH) so $P(\text{two heads}) = \dfrac{3}{8}$.

F.   The Counting Principle

The *counting principle* is a theorem which enables you to bypass the tree diagram and quickly determine how many ways an event can occur. A tree diagram not only tells you how many ways something can occur, but also lists all of the possibilities. The counting principle does not give you a list of the actual events in the sample space. However, the counting principle is much quicker to use than tree diagrams.

In a nutshell, if there are x ways an event can occur and y ways that another event can occur, then the total number of ways x and y can occur will be xy.

The counting principle can also be extended to calculating probabilities themselves. In general, if the probability of an event E occurring is m and the probability of another event F occurring given that E occurred is n, the the probability of both E and F occurring is mn.

Examples:

1.   How many possible outcomes are there for a coin which is tossed four times?

   For each flip of the coin, there are 2 outcomes, namely heads and tails. The counting principle says that if a coin is flipped four times the total number of outcomes will be $2 \times 2 \times 2 \times 2 = 16$.

2.   Mr. Smith needs to go from Baltimore to New York via Philadelphia. There are 6 roads that go from Baltimore to Philadelphia, and there are 8 roads that go between Philadelphia and New York. How many possible different routes can Mr. Smith take?

   Using the counting principle, $6 \times 8 = 48$ different routes.

3.   What is the probability of drawing two aces from a deck of 52 cards?
   This problem requires us to extend the counting principle. We now have more than one probability in question. The probability of drawing the first ace is $\dfrac{4}{52}$.

   The probability of drawing the second ace is a bit harder to determine. After the first ace is drawn, there are only 3 aces left in the deck. Furthermore, since the first ace was drawn, there are only 51 cards left to choose from. The probability of drawing the second ace is therefore $\frac{3}{51}$. From the counting principle $\left(\frac{2}{52}\right) \times \left(\frac{3}{51}\right) = \frac{6}{2,652}$ or $\frac{1}{442}$.

G. Permutations versus Combinations

Many problems in probability deal with choosing x items out of a group of y items. This is where the formulas for permutations and combinations become useful. When the order of the items selected is important, then we are counting *permutations*. If the order is not important, then we are counting *combinations*. In this chapter, the problems deal entirely with permutations.

When using permutations, there is a mathematical symbol which is frequently used. That is the "!" symbol, which stands for "factorial." $n!$ means the product of n and all positive integers less than n. For example:

6! (read "six factorial") $= 6 \times 5 \times 4 \times 3 \times 2 \times 1 = 720$

$10! = 10 \times 9 \times 8 \times 7 \times 6 \times 5 \times 4 \times 3 \times 2 \times 1 = 3,628,800$

There is one more necessary piece of information needed to work with factorials. By definition (so that our formulas work) we define 0! to be equal to 1.

The number of permutations of n things taken r at a time, denoted $_nP_r$, is equal to $\frac{n!}{(n-r)!}$. The number of permutations of n things when all n are taken at a time is $n(n-1) \ldots 3 \cdot 2 \cdot 1 = n!$ This is consistent with the formula for $_nP_r$ which equals $_nP_n = \frac{n!}{(n-n)!} = \frac{n!}{0!} = n!$ Whenever n different items are all permuted, the number of permutations is $n!$ This will be explained in the examples below.

Examples

1. How many arrangements can be made from the letters in the word *DOGS*?

   There are four letters, and we are using all four of them. The number of permutations is $4! = 4 \times 3 \times 2 \times 1 = 24$.

   So there are 24 arrangements of the word *DOGS*.

2. How many three-letter "words" can be made out of the word *MOVIES*?

    There are 6 letters to be chosen from, and they will be chosen and pemuted in groups of 3. In this case, $n = 6$ and $r = 3$. So using our formula:

    $$_6P_3 = \frac{6!}{(6-3)!} = \frac{6!}{3!} = \frac{6 \times 5 \times 4 \times 3 \times 2 \times 1}{3 \times 2 \times 1} = 6 \times 5 \times 4 = 120$$

    So there are 120 ways in which to make three-letter "words" out of the word *MOVIES*.

Questions

1. What is the probability of drawing an ace from a poker deck?

2. What is the probability of rolling a die and getting a prime number?

3. What is the probability of drawing a face card from a poker deck?

4. An urn contains 3 green balls, 4 red balls, and 5 black balls. What is the probability of drawing:

   a. a green ball?
   b. a red ball?
   c. a black ball?

5. There are 15 boys and 20 girls in the classroom. If you choose one student at random, what is the probability you have chosen a girl?

6. The numbers 1 through 10 are written on slips of paper and put in a hat. What is the probability that a number drawn will be even?

7. Using the scenario in problem number 6, what is the probability that the number chosen will be divisible by 3?

8. The numbers 1 through 15 are written on slips of paper and put in a hat. What is the probability that the number drawn will have two digits?

9. What is the probability that the number chosen in problem 8 is an even number?

10. There are 4 pennies, 4 nickels, 5 dimes, and 2 quarters in my pocket. If I reach in and pull out a coin at random, what is the probability that:

    a. I pull out a penny?
    b. I pull out a coin worth over 5 cents?
    c. I pull out a quarter?

11. A Roulette wheel has 38 slots for a ball to roll into when it is spun. These slots are numbered 1−36; in addition, there are slots labeled 0 and 00. If the roulette wheel is spun once, what is the probability that the following will occur:

    a. the ball lands on an even number, not counting 0 or 00?
    b. the ball lands on 0?
    c. the ball lands on one of the numbers 1 through 10?
    d. the ball lands on a prime number?

12. One card is drawn from a set of 52 poker cards. What is the probability that the card is a Jack and a spade?

13. What is the probability that the card drawn from a poker deck is red and a face card?

14. The numbers 1 through 20 are written down an separate pieces of paper and put into a hat. What is the probability that the number chosen is prime and has two digits?

15. In problem 14, what is the probability that the number is divisible by three and has two digits?

16. What is the probability of drawing a diamond or a face card from the standard 52 card deck?

17. What is the probability of drawing a king or a queen from a deck of 52 cards?

18. I have 50 cards. Twenty are red, twenty are yellow, 5 are black, and 5 are blue. I pick one of the cards. What is the probability that:

    a. it is yellow or black?
    b. it is red or yellow?
    c. it is not red or it is black?

19. Bill and Jane's chances of hitting a target with their bows and arrows are $\frac{1}{3}$ and $\frac{3}{4}$, respectively. Both fire at the same target at the same time. Find the probability that:

    a. Bill hits the target and Jane misses.
    b. both miss the target.
    c. both hit the target.
    d. Bill or Jane hits the target.

20. In a certain school, 20 percent of all students have defective eyesight, 30 percent have defective hearing, and 4 percent have both defective eyesight and hearing. Find the probability that:

    a. a child chosen at random does not have defective hearing.
    b. a child chosen at random does not have defective eyesight.
    c. a child chosen at random does not have either defective eyesight or hearing.

Create a tree diagram showing the sample space for the following scenarios:

21. Flipping a coin four times.

Using this tree diagram from the previous problem, answer the following probability question.

22. What is the probability of getting at least 3 heads on four flips of a coin?

23. There are six airlines that travel from Philadelphia to San Francisco. How many distinct ways can a person select the airlines for a round trip if she cannot travel both ways by the same airline?

24. Referring to question 23, how many ways can a person select her round trip if she is allowed to take the same airline to San Francisco and back?

25. A student takes courses in English, Math, Science, History, Phys. Ed., and Art. If the student can get an A, B, C, D, or F in each class, then how many different report cards can be given?

26. Evaluate the following:

    a. $_6P_6$
    b. $_5P_1$
    c. $_8P_4$
    d. $_6P_2$
    e. $_{50}P_{49}$

27. How many ways are there to arrange 5 books on a shelf?

28. How many different ways are there to arrange the numerals 1,2,3,4?

29. How many different 3 digit numbers can be made from 1,2,3,4,7,8,9?

30. How many different lineups can a manager make for his baseball team if he has 12 players and there are 9 players in a lineup? (Hint: in a lineup, order does matter.)

Answers

1. There are 4 aces in the poker deck, so
$$P(\text{ace}) = \frac{4}{52} = \frac{1}{13}.$$

2. The prime numbers between 1 and 6 are 2, 3, and 5. So $P(\text{prime}) = \frac{3}{6} = \frac{1}{2}.$

3. There are four jacks, four queens, and four kings in a poker deck, so $P(\text{face card})$
$$= \frac{12}{52} = \frac{3}{13}.$$

4. There are 12 balls total to choose from, so 12 is the denominator in all the answers.

   a. There are 3 green balls, so $P(\text{green})$
   $$= \frac{3}{12} = \frac{1}{4}.$$

   b. There are 4 red balls, so $P(\text{red})$
   $$= \frac{4}{12} = \frac{1}{3}.$$

   c. There are 5 black balls, so $P(\text{black})$
   $$= \frac{5}{12}.$$

5. There are 35 students in all to choose from, and 20 of them are girls, so $P(\text{girl})$
$$= \frac{20}{35} = \frac{4}{7}.$$

6. Out of the numbers 1 through 10, 5 are even, {2, 4, 6, 8, and 10}, so $P(\text{even})$
$$= \frac{5}{10} = \frac{1}{2}.$$

7. There are 3 numbers that are divisible by {3, 3, 6, and 9}, so $P(\text{divisible by 3})$
$$= \frac{3}{10}.$$

8. Out of the numbers 1 through 15, there are 6 numbers which have 2 digits, {10, 11, 12, 13, 14, and 15}, so $P(\text{2 digit}) =$
$$\frac{6}{15} = \frac{2}{5}.$$

9. There are 7 even numbers between 1 and 15, {2, 4, 6, 8, 10, 12, and 14}, so
$$P(\text{even}) = \frac{7}{15}.$$

10. There are 15 coins in all, so 15 will be the denominator of all the answers.

    a. There are 4 pennies, so $P(\text{penny}) = \frac{4}{15}.$

    b. There are 7 coins worth over 5 cents (the 5 dimes and the 2 quarters), so
    $$P(> 5 \text{ cents}) = \frac{7}{15}.$$

    c. There are 2 quarters, so $P(\text{quarter})$
    $$= \frac{2}{15}.$$

11. There are a grand total of 38 spaces on the roulette wheel, so every denominator will be 38.

    a. Not counting "0" and "00" leaves 18 even numbers, so $P(\text{even}) = \frac{18}{38} = \frac{9}{19}$.

    b. Since there is only one "0" space on the wheel, $P(0) = \frac{1}{38}$.

    c. There are 10 favorable outcomes (the numbers 1 through 10), so $P(1 \text{ through } 10) = \frac{10}{38} = \frac{5}{19}$.

    d. There are 11 prime numbers between 1 and {36, 2, 3, 5, 7, 11, 13, 17, 19, 23, 29, and 31}, so $P(\text{Prime}) = \frac{11}{38}$.

12. There are four jacks, and 13 spades, but there is only one card that fits both categories, so $P(\text{jack and spade}) = \frac{1}{52}$.

    If we let $P(\text{jack}) = \frac{4}{52}$ and $P(\text{spade} \mid \text{jack}) = \frac{1}{4}$ (since only one out of the four jacks are spades), then $P(\text{spade and jack}) = \left(\frac{4}{52}\right)\left(\frac{1}{4}\right) = \frac{1}{52}$.

13. There are 26 red cards (the 13 hearts and the 13 diamonds) and 12 face cards (four jacks, four queens, and four kings), but only 6 cards fit both categories (jack, queen, and king of hearts as well as the jack, queen, and king of diamonds), so $P(\text{red and face card}) = \frac{6}{52} = \frac{3}{26}$.

If we let $P(\text{red}) = \frac{26}{52}$ or $\frac{1}{2}$ and $P(\text{face} \mid \text{red}) = \frac{6}{26}$ or $\frac{3}{13}$ (since there are only 6 red face cards in the 26 we now have after eliminating the black cards), then $P(\text{red and a face card}) = \left(\frac{1}{2}\right)\left(\frac{3}{13}\right) = \frac{3}{26}$.

14. Looking at a list of prime numbers, the ones that fit the "and" category of prime and two digits are 11, 13, 17, and 19, so $P(\text{prime and 2 digits}) = \frac{4}{20} = \frac{1}{5}$.

    If we let $P(\text{prime}) = \frac{8}{20}$ and $P(2 \text{ digits} \mid \text{prime}) = \frac{4}{8}$ (since only 4 of the 8 prime numbers have 2 digits in them), then $P(\text{prime and 2 digits}) = \left(\frac{8}{20}\right)\left(\frac{4}{8}\right) = \frac{4}{20} = \frac{1}{5}$.

15. There are only 3 numbers that have two digits and are divisible by {3, 12, 15, and 18}, so $P(\text{divisible by 3 and 2 digits}) = \frac{3}{20}$.

    If we let $P(2 \text{ digits}) = \frac{10}{20}$ or $\frac{1}{2}$ and $P(\text{divisible by 3}) = \frac{3}{10}$ (since only 3 out of the remaining 10 are divisible by 3), then $P(2 \text{ digits and divisible by 3}) = \left(\frac{1}{2}\right)\left(\frac{3}{10}\right) = \frac{3}{20}$.

16. $P(\text{diamond or face}) = P(\text{diamond}) + P(\text{face}) - P(\text{diamond and face})$

$$= \frac{13}{52} + \frac{12}{52} - \frac{3}{52}$$

$$= \frac{22}{52} = \frac{11}{26}$$

17. $P(\text{king or queen}) = P(\text{king}) + P(\text{queen}) - P(\text{king and queen})$

$$= \frac{4}{52} + \frac{4}{52} - \frac{0}{52}$$

$$= \frac{8}{52} = \frac{2}{13}$$

18. a. $P(\text{yellow or black}) = P(\text{yellow}) + P(\text{black}) - P(\text{yellow and black})$

$$= \frac{20}{50} + \frac{5}{50} - \frac{0}{50}$$

$$= \frac{25}{50} \text{ or } \frac{1}{2}$$

  b. $P(\text{red or yellow}) = P(\text{red}) + P(\text{yellow}) - P(\text{red and yellow})$

$$= \frac{20}{50} + \frac{20}{50} - \frac{0}{50}$$

$$= \frac{40}{50} \text{ or } \frac{4}{5}$$

  c. For this problem, we must figure out what it means to be not red. Since there are 20 red cards, then any other card will fit the category "not red." Also, we will have an overlap for the *and* part of our probability formula.

  $P(\text{not red or black}) = P(\text{not red}) + P(\text{black}) - P(\text{not red and black})$

$$= \frac{30}{50} + \frac{5}{50} - \frac{5}{50}$$

$$= \frac{30}{50} \text{ or } \frac{3}{5}$$

19. First, list the individual probabilities needed for this problem:

$$P(\text{Bill hits the target}) = \frac{1}{3}$$

$$P(\text{Bill misses the target}) = 1 - \frac{1}{3} = \frac{2}{3}$$

$$P(\text{Jane hits the target}) = \frac{3}{4}$$

$$P(\text{Jane misses the target}) = 1 - \frac{3}{4} = \frac{1}{4}$$

  a. $P(\text{Bill hits and Jane misses}) = P(\text{Bill hits}) \, P(\text{Jane misses})$

$$= \left(\frac{1}{3}\right)\left(\frac{1}{4}\right)$$

$$= \frac{1}{12}$$

  b. $P(\text{Bill and Jane miss}) = P(\text{Bill misses}) \, P(\text{Jane misses})$

$$= \left(\frac{2}{3}\right)\left(\frac{1}{4}\right)$$

$$= \frac{2}{12} \text{ or } \frac{1}{6}$$

  c. $P(\text{Bill and Jane hit}) = P(\text{Bill hits}) \, P(\text{Jane hits})$

$$= \left(\frac{1}{3}\right)\left(\frac{3}{4}\right)$$

$$= \frac{3}{12} \text{ or } \frac{1}{4}$$

  d. $P(\text{Bill or Jane hits}) = P(\text{Bill hits}) + P(\text{Jane hits}) - P(\text{Bill and Jane hit})$

$$= \frac{1}{3} + \frac{3}{4} - \frac{1}{4} \text{ (the } \frac{1}{4} \text{ is from part c)}$$

$$= \frac{5}{6}$$

20. First we'll list the probabilities we may need

    P(defective eyesight) $= 0.2$

    P(defective hearing) $= 0.3$

    P(defective eyesight and defective hearing) $= 0.04$

    a. P(not defective hearing) $= 1 -$ P(defective hearing) $= 1 - .3 = .7$ or 70 percent

    b. P(not defective eyesight) $= 1 -$ P(defective eyesight) $= 1 - .2 = .8$ or 80 percent

    c. P(defective eyesight) $= 0.2$

    P(defective hearing) $= 0.3$

    P(defective eyesight and hearing) $= 0.4$

    P(defective eyesight or hearing) $=$

    P(defective eyesight) $+$ P(defective hearing) $-$ P(defective eyesight and hearing)

    P(defective eyesight or defective hearing) $= 0.3 + 0.2 - 0.04 = 0.46$

    P(Not defective eyesight and not defective hearing) $=$

    $1 -$ P(defective eyesight or defective hearing) $= 1 - 0.46 = 0.54$

21.

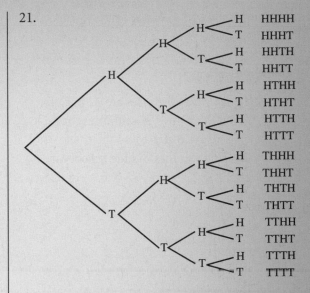

22. By counting from the tree diagram, we see that there are 16 ways that a coin can be flipped four times. The ways that come up with at least 3 heads are {HHHH, HHHT, HHTH, HTHH, and THHH}, so P(at least 3 heads) $= \dfrac{5}{16}$.

23. From Philadelphia to San Francisco there are 6 airlines she can select. If she cannot take the same airline back, then there are only 5 airlines she can take for the return trip. By the counting principle, the number of ways she can accomplish the round trip is $6 \times 5 = 30$.

24. If she is allowed to make a return trip on the same airline, then the change from problem 23 is that she has 6 ways, not five, to make the return trip. $6 \times 6 = 36$.

25. If the grades for all classes are A, B, C, D, or F, then there are 5 possibilities for each class. There are 6 classes, so the total number of different possible report cards will be $5 \times 5 \times 5 \times 5 \times 5 \times 5 = 15{,}625$.

26. a.

$$_6P_6 \; = \; \frac{6!}{(6-6)!}$$

$$= \; \frac{6!}{0!}$$

$$= \; \frac{720}{1} \; (0! = 1 \text{ by definition})$$

$$= \; 720$$

 b.
$$_5P_1 \; = \; \frac{5!}{(5-1)!}$$

$$= \; \frac{5!}{4!}$$

$$= \; \frac{120}{24}$$

$$= \; 5$$

 c.
$$_8P_4 \; = \; \frac{8!}{(8-4)!}$$

$$= \; \frac{8!}{4!}$$

$$= \; \frac{8 \times 7 \times 6 \times 5 \times 4 \times 3 \times 2 \times 1}{4 \times 3 \times 2 \times 1}$$

$$= \; 8 \times 7 \times 6 \times 5$$

$$= \; 1{,}680$$

 d.
$$_6P_2 \; = \; \frac{6!}{(6-2)!}$$

$$= \; \frac{6!}{4!}$$

$$= \; \frac{6 \times 5 \times 4 \times 3 \times 2 \times 1}{4 \times 3 \times 2 \times 1}$$

$$= \; 6 \times 5$$

$$= \; 30$$

 e.
$$_{50}P_{49} \; = \; \frac{50!}{(50-49)!}$$

$$= \; \frac{50!}{1!}$$

$$= \; \frac{50!}{1}$$

$$= \; 50!$$

27. The number of arrangements on a shelf is a permutation. Since there are 5 books and we are using all 5 at a time, we need to compute 5!.

$$5! = 5 \times 4 \times 3 \times 2 \times 1 = 120$$

There are 120 ways of arranging the 5 books.

28. The number of ways to permute the 4 numbers is

$$4! = 4 \times 3 \times 2 \times 1 = 24$$

29. There are 7 numbers to be chosen from and they will be chosen and permuted in groups of 3. In this case $n = 7$ and $r = 3$. So using our formula:

$$_7P_3 = \frac{7!}{(7-3)!} = \frac{7!}{4!}$$

$$7! = \frac{7 \times 6 \times 5 \times 4 \times 3 \times 2 \times 1}{4 \times 3 \times 2 \times 1}$$

$$7 \times 6 \times 5 \times 1 = 210$$

30. There are 12 players to be chosen from and they will be chosen and permuted in groups of 9. In this case $n = 12$ and $r = q$. So using our formula:

$$_{12}P_9 = \frac{12!}{(12-9)!} = \frac{12!}{3!}$$

Chapter 7

Statistics

A. Collecting and organizing data

Statistics is a branch of mathematics which concerns itself with simplifying, reading, and interpreting data. This data could be the results of a survey of favorite TV shows, your class grades, or car insurance rates.

The first step in analyzing data is to collect and organize it. Each problem is different and there is often more than one way to organize the data efficiently. We will discuss a few methods of data organization here. For our first example, consider the grades of 30 students on their final exams. When originally collected and written down, the data appeared as follows:

55%	97%	87%	76%	62%	99%
76%	100%	65%	52%	89%	89%
67%	81%	83%	91%	78%	77%
80%	50%	67%	84%	99%	95%
77%	70%	90%	77%	92%	84%

B. Tallies and frequency tables

The first decision we must make in organizing this data is to decide how to group it. We need to make all of this data we collected a little more compact so it will be easier to understand. Let's create intervals consisting of every 10 points. A *tally* would then look like this:

INTERVAL	# in that interval
91–100	////////
81–90	/////////
71–80	////////
61–70	/////
51–60	//
41–50	/

The table above takes intervals and indicates how many pieces of data fit into each interval. If we actually write down how many pieces of data there are in each interval, we will have created a *frequency table*:

INTERVAL	# in that interval
91–100	7
81–90	8
71–80	7
61–70	5
51–60	2
41–50	1

C. Histograms

A histogram is a way of showing the data you've collected and organized in a chart format. There are two kinds of histograms discussed here. One is a frequency histogram. The other is a cumulative frequency histogram.

A *frequency histogram* is a graph of the data in a frequency table. The horizontal axis contains the intervals and the vertical axis shows the frequency.

A *cumulative frequency histogram* depicts a running total of the frequencies.

Example:

1. Use the test score data and its frequency to make a frequency histogram and a cumulative frequency histogram.

55%	97%	87%	76%	62%	99%
76%	100%	65%	52%	89%	89%
67%	81%	83%	91%	78%	77%
80%	50%	67%	84%	99%	95%
77%	70%	90%	77%	92%	84%

INTERVAL	# in that interval
91–100	7
81–90	8
71–80	7
61–70	5
51–60	2
under 50	1

The intervals will be placed along the horizontal axis and rectangles will be drawn to show how many data points are in each interval. These rectangles touch each other.

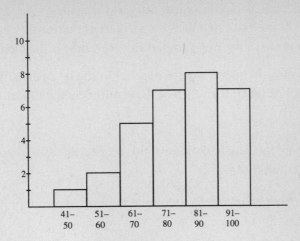

In a cumulative frequency histogram, the frequency associated with each interval is the total of the frequencies of all intervals up to that point.

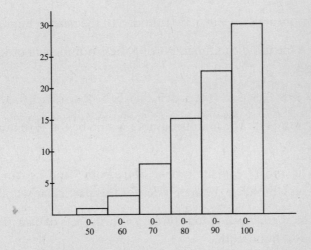

D. Measures of central tendency

A *measure of central tendency* is a number that tells something about the way the set of data is centered. There are three types of measures of central tendency that we will discuss: the median, the mean, and the mode.

The *mean* is what most people refer to as the *average*. To find the mean, add up all the data values and divide by the number of pieces of data.

The *median* is the middle number. If you take a set of data with an odd number of data points, and arrange it in order from largest to smallest (or vice versa), the number that appears in the exact middle is the median. If there are an even number of data points, then the mean of the two numbers in the middle is the median.

The *mode* is the most frequently found number in the set of data. If there is a "tie" for the most frequent number, then each of those numbers is a mode for that set of data.

Examples:

1. Find the mean, median, and mode of this set of data. Round your answers off to the nearest hundredth.

4	3	9	6	9	8	3	5	4	1	0	4
3	5	2	9	8	5	7	6	1	5	6	8
9	7	5	4	3	9	8					

   The mean is calculated by adding up the numbers and dividing by the number of numbers. The sum of the numbers is 166. There are 31 numbers in the set of data.

   Therefore, the mean is $\frac{166}{31} = 5.35$ (rounded to the nearest hundredth)

   The median is the middle number. Putting these numbers in order from greatest to least, we get:

   9, 9, 9, 9, 9, 8, 8, 8, 8, 7, 7, 6, 6, 6, 5, 5, 5, 5, 5, 4, 4, 4, 4, 3, 3, 3, 3, 2, 1, 1, 0

   There are 31 numbers. The middle number would be the 16th number in the list, which is 5.

   The mode is the most frequent number. Since both 9 and 5 occur in our data equally (5 times), both 5 and 9 are modes for this particular set of data.

2. Find the mean, median, and mode of the following sets of data. Round all answers off to the nearest hundredth.

   43 96 98 35 41 04 35 29 85 76 15 68

   97 54 39 86

   Mean $= \frac{901}{16} = 56.31$

Median—Since there are 16 pieces of data, there is no true middle number. Take the two numbers closest to the middle and compute their mean to find the median.

04, 15, 29, 35, 35, 39, 41, **43**, **54**, 68, 76, 85, 86, 96, 97, 98

$$\frac{43 + 54}{2} = 48.5 \text{ is the median}$$

Mode—the number 35 occurs most frequently, so the mode is 35.

E.   Other statistical measures

There are two other statistical measures that it is important to understand at this time.

Range—The *range* of a set of data is a number showing the "spread" of the data. The range is simply the difference between the highest and lowest data values.

Percentiles—A *percentile* is the piece of data such that a particular percent of the data falls at or below. The data value which is the 70th percentile indicates that 70 percent of all the data falls at or below that value. The common percentiles 25 percent, 50 percent, and 75 percent are given the special name of *quartiles*. The first quartile is the 25th percentile, the second quartile is the 50th percentile, and the 3rd quartile is the 75th percentile. The second quartile is also the median of that set of data. Sometimes the first quartile is called the lower quartile, the 3rd quartile the upper quartile, and the 50th percentile the middle quartile.

Examples:

1.   Find the range, the first quartile, and the 70th percentile for the set of below.

55%	97%	87%	76%	62%	99%
76%	100%	65%	52%	89%	89%
67%	81%	83%	91%	78%	77%
80%	50%	67%	84%	99%	95%
77%	70%	90%	77%	92%	84%

Searching through the data, we see the highest score is a 100 percent and the lowest score is 50 percent. Therefore the range of this set of data is $100 - 50 = 50$.

To find quartiles (or any other percentile) you must order the data just as you did to find the median. By multiplying the percentile by the number of pieces of data, you will get the number of the term you're looking for.

There are 30 terms in our data. Put in order from least to greatest we get:

50, 52, 55, 62, 65, 67, 67, 70, 76, 76, 77, 77, 77, 78, 80, 81, 83, 84, 84, 87, 89, 89, 90, 91, 92, 95, 97, 99, 99, 100

In order to find the lower quartile, multiply the number of items you have by 25 percent. This will give you the term you're looking for.

$(30)(.25) = 7.5$

Always round the result up to the next whole number, in this case 8. Remember that we are trying to find the position of the piece of data below which everything else will fall. Now find the eighth term on the list:

50, 52, 55, 62, 65, 67, 67, **70**, 76, 76, 77, 77, 77, 78, 80, 81, 83, 84, 84, 87, 89, 89, 90, 91, 92, 95, 97, 99, 99, 100

So 70 is the first quartile in our data.

Multiplying $(30)(.7) = 21$, so the 21st number on our list is the 70th percentile. That number is 89.

Questions

55%	97%	87%	76%	62%	99%
76%	100%	65%	52%	89%	89%
67%	81%	83%	91%	78%	77%
80%	50%	67%	84%	99%	95%
77%	70%	90%	77%	92%	84%

1. Using the chart of test scores above, create a tally with an interval of every 5 points.

2. Using your results from problem 1, write down the frequency table for your data.

3. Choose an interval and create a tally and frequency chart for the following set of data:

   12 36 43 94 56 66 73 55 92 82 99
   65 10 03 95 89 67 58 94 32 87 31
   68 74 37 69 85 67 86 75 89 89 75
   43 78 65 43 67 54

4. Using the same data from problem 3, create another frequency chart using an interval different from the one you used in problem 3.

5. Create a tally and a frequency table for this set of data. Let the interval be 25.

154	287	187	154	137	252
243	176	157	164	235	172
289	277	165	119	154	238
165	156	249	157	199	156
247	282	143	298	189	213
176	244	200	119	170	233
214	177	298	199	103	192
188	165	232			

6. Draw a frequency histogram and a cumulative frequency histogram using the data that was used in problem 1 of this chapter.

7. Draw a frequency histogram and a cumulative frequency histogram using the data that was used in problem 3 of this chapter.

8. Draw a frequency histogram and a cumulative frequency histogram using the data that was used in problem 5 of this chapter.

Find the mean, mode, and median for each set of data given. Round your answers off to the hundredths place if necessary.

9. 28 70 16 99 43 12 65 88 94 62 46
   99 01 72 67 58 98 04 87

10.
189	223	140	187	190	191
204	138	196	172	231	154
134	189	165	140	186	193
124	167	163	155	167	208
195	137	142	136	224	175
149	186	158	195	147	

11. 4 5 8 6 7 7 3 6 2 5 3 8

12. 16 17 15 19 17 18 14 14 14 14 16
    15 19 18 17 14 16 15 18 17 16 13
    15 11 14 16 15 17 19 17 16 15 16
    18 17 19 18 10 19 18 17 16 15 17

13. 1,956 1,940 1,932 1,989 1,957 1,923
    1,956 1,947 1,960 1,901

14.
55%	97%	87%	76%	62%	99%
76%	100%	65%	52%	89%	89%
67%	81%	83%	91%	78%	77%
80%	50%	67%	84%	99%	95%
77%	70%	90%	77%	92%	84%

15. 154   287   187   154   137   252
     243   176   157   164   235   172
     289   277   165   119   154   238
     165   156   249   157   199

16. 82   73   65   92   31   87
     23   76   105   48   65   79
     89   80   114   08   91   87
     65   76   57   54   32   80
     110   96   86   89   70   18

17. 12   36   43   94   56   66
     73   55   92   82   99   65
     10   03   95   89   67   58
     94   32   87   31   68   74
     37   69   85   67   86   75
     89   89   75   43   78   65
     43   67   54

18. 78   66   100   97   85   85
     94   76   86   90   72   55
     91   74   72   77   79   75
     81   93   74   76   77   77
     80   60   63   88   95   95
     71   67   68

19. Find the range of this set of data from problem 13.

     1956   1940   1932   1989   1957   1923
     1956   1947   1960   1901

20. Find the 10th and 90th percentiles from this set of test scores from an earlier example.

     55%   97%   87%   76%   62%   99%
     76%   100%   65%   52%   89%   89%
     67%   81%   83%   91%   78%   77%
     80%   50%   67%   84%   99%   95%
     77%   70%   90%   77%   92%   84%

21. Find the range and the quartiles for this set of data from problem 9.

     28   70   16   99   43   12
     65   88   94   62   46   99
     01   72   67   58   98   04
     87

22. Find the range, the 20th percentile, and the 90th percentile for this set of data from problem 10.

     189   223   140   187   190   191
     204   138   196   172   231   154
     134   189   165   140   186   193
     124   167   163   155   167   208
     195   137   142   136   224   175
     149   186   158   195   147

23. Find the quartiles for this set of data from problem 11.

     4   5   8   6   7   7   3   6   2   5   3   8

24. Find the 70th, 80th, and 95th percentile for this set of data from problem 12.

     16   17   15   19   17   18
     14   14   14   14   16   15
     19   18   17   14   16   15
     18   17   16   13   15   11
     14   16   15   17   19   17
     16   15   16   18   17   19
     18   10   19   18   17   16
     15   17

25. Find the range, the lower quartile, and the upper quartile for this set of data from problem 15.

     154   287   187   154   137   252
     243   176   157   164   235   172
     289   277   165   119   154   238
     165   156   249   157   199

26. Find the 30th, 60th, and 90th percentile for this set of data from problem 16.

82	73	65	92	31	87
23	76	105	48	65	79
89	80	114	08	91	87
65	76	57	54	32	80
110	96	86	89	70	18

27. Find the range, the 15th percentile, and the 95th percentile for this set of data from problem 17.

12	36	43	94	56	66
73	55	92	82	99	65
10	03	95	89	67	58
94	32	87	31	68	74
37	69	85	67	86	75
89	89	75	43	78	65
43	67	54			

28. Find the range and the quartiles for this set of data from problem 18.

78	66	100	97	85	85
94	76	86	90	72	55
91	74	72	77	79	75
81	93	74	76	77	77
80	60	63	88	95	95
71	67	68			

Answers

1. Knowing that the scores range from 50 to 100, let's make the first interval 96 to 100 and work down from there. Then we can make the tally.

Interval	Tally
96–100	////
91–95	///
86–90	////
81–85	////
76–80	////////
71–75	
66–70	///
61–65	//
56–60	
51–55	//
46–50	/

2. Using the data from the tally in problem 1, write in the actual number of pieces of data in each interval to create the frequency table.

Interval	Frequency
96–100	4
91–95	3
86–90	4
81–85	4
76–80	7
71–75	
66–70	3
61–65	2
56–60	
51–55	2
46–50	1

3. Answers will vary. Here, we have created a tally and a frequency table using an interval of 10.

Interval	Tally	Frequency
90–99	/////	5
80–89	////////	7
70–79	/////	5
60–69	/////////	8
50–59	////	4
40–49	///	3
30–39	////	4
20–29		
10–19	//	2
0–9	/	1

4. Again, answers will vary. The solution here has an interval of 20.

Interval	Frequency
80–99	12
60–79	13
40–59	7
20–39	4
0–19	3

5. The values range from the low 100s to the upper 200s. Since there is no number in the 300 range, we have started our intervals with 275–299. You could have started with 276–300 as your first interval. Doing that will result in a different table. Again, we combine the tally and the frequency table into one chart:

Interval	Tally	Frequency
275–299	//////	6
250–274	/	1
225–249	////////	8
200–224	///	3
175–199	/////////	9
150–174	/////////////	13
125–149	//	2
100–124	///	3

6. Using the frequency table from problem 1:

Interval	Frequency
96–100	4
91–95	3
86–90	4
81–85	4
76–80	7
71–75	
66–70	3
61–65	2
56–60	
51–55	2
46–50	1

First we create a frequency histogram using the intervals for the horizontal axis and labeling the vertical axis to at least 7, since 7 is the largest frequency.

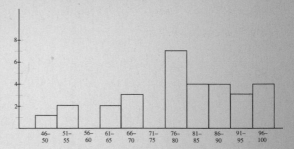

Second, to create a cumulative frequency histogram, the vertical axis must be marked to at least 30. The first category will be the interval 46–50. The next interval will be from 46–55, then 46–60, etcetera, until we reach the final category of 46–100.

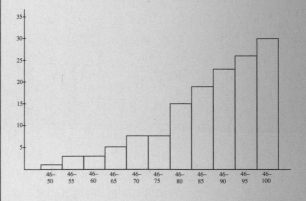

7. Your frequency chart could be different from the one we used. Your histograms could also look different. Using the frequency chart we developed in problem 3:

Interval	Tally	Frequency
90–99	/////	5
80–89	////////	7
70–79	/////	5
60–69	////////	8
50–59	////	4
40–49	///	3
30–39	////	4
20–29		
10–19	//	2
0–9	/	1

Setting up the horizontal axis with the intervals and labeling the vertical axis to 8, we can draw the frequency histogram.

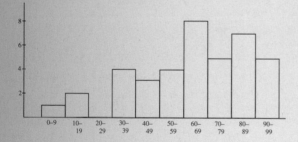

Then starting with the intervals 0–9, 0–19, 0–29, etcetera, we can make the cumulative frequency histogram. The vertical axis must go to at least 39 since there are 39 pieces of data in total.

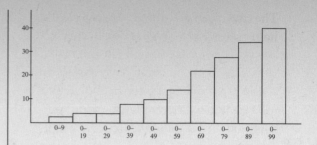

8. Using the frequency table from problem 5, we set up our axes in the same fashion as in problems 6 and 7.

Interval	frequency
275–299	6
250–274	1
225–249	8
200–224	3
175–199	9
150–174	13
125–149	2
100–124	3

The frequency histogram must have its vertical axis labeled to at least 13.

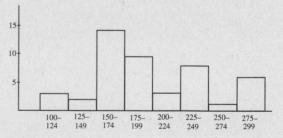

The cumulative frequency histogram must have its vertical axis labeled to at least 45.

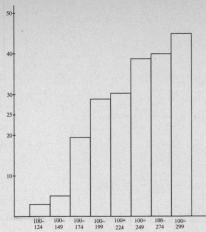

9. Mean—There are 19 numbers and their sum is 1,109. The mean, therefore, is $\frac{1109}{19} = 58.37$.

Median—Putting the data in order from lowest to highest gives us the following list:

1, 4, 12, 16, 28, 43, 46, 58, 62, 65, 67, 70, 72, 87, 88, 94, 98, 99, 99

65 is the number in the middle of the list, so 65 is the median. The median can also be found by dividing 19 (the number of terms) by 2. The result is 9.5, which rounds to 10. The tenth term, counting from either direction, is the median. This technique works when there are an odd number of pieces of data.

Mode—By inspection, the number 99 is listed more than any other number (twice). Therefore, 99 is the mode.

10. Mean—There are 35 terms and their sum is 6,050. The mean is $\frac{6,050}{35} = 172.86$.
Median—Putting all 35 terms in order gives us:
124, 134, 136, 137, 138, 140, 140, 142, 147, 149, 154, 155, 158, 163, 165, 167, 167, 172, 175, 186, 186, 187, 189, 189, 190, 191, 193, 195, 195, 196, 204, 208, 223, 224, 231

$\frac{35}{2} = 17.5$, which rounds to 18. The 18th number on the list is 172.

Mode—There are 5 modes. The numbers 140, 167, 186, 189, and 195 are all listed twice.

11. Mean—There are 12 numbers and their sum is 64. $\frac{64}{12} = 5.33$.

Median—Putting the numbers in order yields

2, 3, 3, 4, 5, 5, 6, 6, 7, 7, 8, 8.

There is no true middle number since the number of pieces of data is even. Take the two terms closest to the middle and find their mean. $\frac{5+6}{2} = 5.5$.

Modes—There are 5 modes. The numbers 3, 5, 6, 7, and 8 are all listed twice.

12. Mean—There are 44 pieces of data and their sum is 707. $\frac{707}{44} = 16.07$

    Median—Since there are an even number of terms, we take the two nearest the middle. This time, however, they are both the same number 16. So the median is 16.

    The number 17 appears most often (9 times). The mode is 17.

13. Mean—There are 10 numbers and their sum is 19,461. $\frac{19,461}{10} = 1,946.1$

    Median—Finding the mean of the two numbers nearest the middle gives us $\frac{1,947 + 1,956}{2} = 1,951.5$.

    Mode—The mode is 1,956, which appears twice on the list.

14. Mean $= \frac{2,389}{30} = 79.63$

    Median $= \frac{80 + 81}{2} = 80.5$

    Mode $= 77$, which appears 3 times.

15. Mean $= \frac{4,486}{23} = 195.04$.

    Median $= 172$, the 12th term.

    Mode $= 154$ (3 times).

16. Mean $= \frac{2,128}{30} = 70.93$.

    Median $= \frac{76 + 79}{2} = 77.5$.

    Mode $= 65$.

17. Mean $= \frac{2,503}{39} = 64.18$.

    Median $= 67$.

    Modes $= 43, 67,$ and 89.

18. Mean $= \frac{2,617}{33} = 79.30$.

    Median $= 77$.

    Mode $= 77$.

19. The range is calculated by subtracting the lowest score from the highest score. The range here is $1,989 - 1,901 = 88$.

20. We already have put these scores in order from lowest to highest (see above example). Now we multiply the percentile by the number of terms to see which term we are looking for:

    10th percentile = $.10 \times 30 = 3$, or the third lowest score

    90th percentile = $.90 \times 30 = 27$, or the 27th lowest score

    Counting through our sorted list, we find that the third score is 55 percent and the 27th score is 97 percent. So, the 10th percentile is 55 percent and the 90th percentile is 97 percent.

21. The largest number is 99, the smallest number is 1, so the range is $99 - 1 = 98$.

    There are 19 numbers in the survey, so, as we did last problem:

    1st quartile = $.25 \times 19 = 4.75$ or the 5th score

    2nd quartile = $.50 \times 19 = 9.5$ or the 10th score

    3rd quartile = $.75 \times 19 = 14.25$ or the 15th score

    Looking these up on our sorted list, we find the 5th score is 28, the tenth score is 65 (which is also the median), and the 15th score is 88.

22. Range = $231 - 124 = 107$.

    20th percentile = $.20 \times 35 = 7$, the seventh term is 140

    90th percentile = $.90 \times 35 = 31.5$ or 32, the 32nd term is 208

23. 1st quartile = $.25 \times 12 = 3$, the third term is 3

    2nd quartile = median the average of the 6th and 7th terms = $\frac{5+6}{2} = 5.5$

    3rd quartile = $.75 \times 12 = 9$, the 9th term is 7

24. 70th percentile = $.70 \times 44 = 30.8$, or the 31st term, which is 17

    80th percentile = $.80 \times 44 = 35.2$, or the 36th term, which is 18

    95th percentile = $.95 \times 44 = 41.8$, or the 42nd term, which is 19

25. Range = $289 - 119 = 170$

    lower quartile = $.25 \times 23 = 5.75$ or the 6th term which is 156

    upper quartile = $.75 \times 23 = 17.25$ or the 18th term which is 243

26. 30th percentile = $.30 \times 30 = 9$ and the 9th term is 65

    60th percentile = $.60 \times 30 = 18$ and the 18th term is 80

    90th percentile = $.90 \times 30 = 27$ and the 27th term is 96

27. Range = 99 − 3 = 96

    15th percentile = .15 × 39 = 5.85—the 6th term is 36

    95th percentile = .95 × 39 = 37.05—the 38th term is 95

28. Range = 100 − 55 = 45

    1st quartile = .25 × 33 = 8.25—the 9th term is 72

    2nd quartile = .50 × 33 = 16.5—the 17th term is 77

    3rd quartile = .75 × 33 = 24.75—the 25th term is 88

Part IV

Practice Tests and Answers

Practice Test 2

Answer 30 questions from this part. Each correct answer will receive 2 credits. No partial credit will be allowed. Write your answers in the spaces provided on the separate answer sheet. Where applicable, answers may be left in terms of π or in radical form.   [60]

1 Let p represent "The Yankees won last night" and let q represent "The Yankees stayed in first place." Using p and q, write in symbolic form the statement: "If the Yankees did not win last night, then they did not stay in first place."

2 What is the mode of the set of values 25, 35, 35, 35, 45, 55, 85, and 95?

3 In the accompanying diagram, $ABCD$ is a quadrilateral, $AD = x$, $AB = x + 1$, $BC = 9$, and $DC = 2x + 5$. Find the value of x if the perimeter of quadrilateral $ABCD$ is 35.

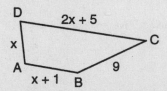

4 In the accompanying diagram, lines $\overleftrightarrow{AB}$, $\overleftrightarrow{CD}$, and $\overrightarrow{EF}$ intersect at G. If m∠DGB = 35 and m∠CGF = 75, find m∠AGE.

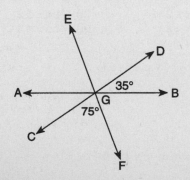

5 In the accompanying diagram, △ABC is similar to △$A'B'C'$, AB = 24, BC = 30, and CA = 40. If the shortest side of △$A'B'C'$ is 6, find the length of the longest side of △$A'B'C'$.

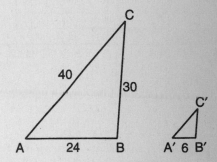

6 In the accompanying diagram, parallel lines $\overleftrightarrow{AB}$ and $\overleftrightarrow{CD}$ are intersected by transversal $\overleftrightarrow{EF}$ at G and H, respectively. If m∠AGH = 4x + 30 and m∠GHD = 7x – 9, what is the value of x?

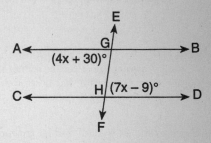

7 Solve for x: $0.4x - 3 = 1.4$

8 Solve for x: $3x + 4 = 5(x - 8)$

9 Express as a trinomial:
$$(2x - 3)(x + 7)$$

153

10 Write, in symbolic form, the inverse of $\sim p \rightarrow \sim q$.

11 In the accompanying diagram, parallelogram $ABCD$ has vertices $A(2,1)$, $B(8,1)$, $C(11,5)$, and $D(5,5)$. What is the area of parallelogram $ABCD$?

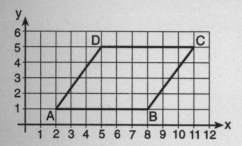

12 What is the slope of the line whose equation is $y = 3x - 5$?

13 If x varies directly as y and $x = 3$ when $y = 8$, find the value of y when $x = 9$.

14 If the legs of a right triangle have measures of 9 and 12, what is the length of the hypotenuse?

15 Express $x^2 - 5x - 24$ as the product of two binomials.

Directions (16–35): For *each* question chosen, write on the separate answer sheet the *numeral* preceding the word or expression that best completes the statement or answers the question.

16 Let p represent "It is cold" and let q represent "It is snowing." Which expression can be used to represent "It is cold and it is not snowing"?

(1) $\sim p \wedge q$ (3) $p \vee \sim q$
(2) $p \wedge \sim q$ (4) $\sim p \vee q$

17 If Manuel has five different shirts and seven different ties, how many different choices of a shirt and a tie does he have?

(1) 5   (3) 12
(2) 7   (4) 35

18 A bag has five green marbles and four blue marbles. If one marble is drawn at random, what is the probability that it is *not* green?

(1) $\frac{1}{9}$ (3) $\frac{5}{9}$
(2) $\frac{4}{9}$ (4) $\frac{5}{20}$

19 If one side of a regular octagon is represented by $2x - 1$, the perimeter of the octagon can be represented by

(1) $12x - 1$ (3) $12x - 6$
(2) $16x - 1$ (4) $16x - 8$

20 The product $\left(\dfrac{2a^3}{5b}\right)\left(\dfrac{3a^2}{7b}\right)$ is

(1) $\dfrac{5a^5}{12b^2}$ (3) $\dfrac{6a^5}{35b^2}$
(2) $\dfrac{5a^6}{12b}$ (4) $\dfrac{6a^6}{35b}$

21 What is the additive inverse of $-4a$?

(1) $\dfrac{a}{4}$ (3) $-\dfrac{4}{a}$
(2) $4a$ (4) $-\dfrac{1}{4a}$

22 Which inequality is represented in the accompanying graph?

(1) $-4 \leq x \leq 2$ (3) $-4 < x \leq 2$
(2) $-4 < x < 2$ (4) $-4 \leq x < 2$

23 The sum of $3\sqrt{5}$ and $6\sqrt{5}$ is

(1) $18\sqrt{5}$ (3) $9\sqrt{10}$
(2) 45 (4) $9\sqrt{5}$

24 For which value of x will the fraction $\dfrac{7}{2x - 6}$ be undefined?

(1) 0   (3) 3
(2) −3   (4) 6

25 Which pair of angles x and y are supplementary?

(1) m∠x = 113
    m∠y = 67

(3) m∠x = 140
    m∠y = 190

(2) m∠x = 76
    m∠y = 14

(4) m∠x = 180
    m∠y = 180

26 The numerical value of the expression $\frac{5!}{3!}$ is

(1) 9
(2) 10

(3) 20
(4) 40

27 If x = 0.6 and y = 5, the value of $2(xy)^3$ is

(1) 5.4
(2) 21.6

(3) 54
(4) 216

28 What is the mean (average) of $4y + 3$ and $2y - 1$?

(1) $3y + 1$
(2) $3y + 2$

(3) $3y + 4$
(4) $y + 1$

29 Which letter has *only* horizontal line symmetry?

(1) A
(2) D

(3) H
(4) F

30 If $x + ay = b$, then y equals

(1) $\dfrac{b - x}{a}$

(3) $b - x - a$

(2) $\dfrac{b}{x + a}$

(4) $\dfrac{b - a}{x}$

31 If $28x^3 - 36x^2 + 4x$ is divided by $4x$, the quotient will be

(1) $7x^2 - 9x$
(2) $28x^3 - 36x^2$

(3) $7x^2 - 9x + 1$
(4) $28x^3 - 36x^2 + 1$

32 What is the length of the radius of a circle whose area is 100π?

(1) 5
(2) 10

(3) 20
(4) 25

33 Expressed as a fraction, the sum of $\dfrac{4y}{5}$ and $\dfrac{3y}{4}$ is equivalent to

(1) $\dfrac{31y}{20}$

(3) $\dfrac{7y}{20}$

(2) $\dfrac{7y}{9}$

(4) $\dfrac{31y}{9}$

34 What is the *negative* value of x that satisfies the equation $2x^2 + 5x - 3 = 0$?

(1) -1

(3) -3

(2) $-\dfrac{1}{2}$

(4) $-\dfrac{2}{3}$

35 In the accompanying diagram, $\triangle R'S'T'$ is the image of $\triangle RST$.

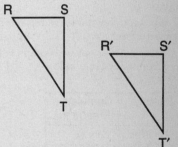

Which type of transformation is shown in this diagram?

(1) dilation
(2) reflection

(3) rotation
(4) translation

Answers to the following questions are to be written on paper provided by the school.

Part II

Answer four questions from this part. Clearly indicate the necessary steps, including appropriate formula substitutions, diagrams, graphs, charts, etc. Calculations that may be obtained by mental arithmetic or the calculator do not need to be shown. [40]

36 The frequency table below shows the distribution of time, in minutes, in which 36 students finished the 5K Firecracker Run.

Interval (minutes)	Frequency
14–16	2
17–19	6
20–22	9
23–25	8
26–28	7
29–31	4

a How many students finished the race in less than 23 minutes? [2]

b Based on the frequency table, which interval contains the median? [2]

c *On your answer paper*, copy and complete the cumulative frequency table below. [2]

Interval	Cumulative Frequency
14–16	2
14–19	
14–22	
14–25	
14–28	
14–31	

d *On graph paper*, using the cumulative frequency table completed in part *c*, construct a cumulative frequency histogram. [4]

37 Let *p* represent: "The stove is hot."
Let *q* represent: "The water is boiling."
Let *r* represent: "The food is cooking."

a Write in symbolic form the converse of the statement: "If the stove is not hot, then the water is not boiling." [2]

b Write in sentence form: $\sim r \rightarrow \sim q$ [2]

c Write in sentence form: $p \lor \sim r$ [2]

d *On your answer paper*, construct a truth table for the statement $p \land \sim q$. [4]

38 In the accompanying diagram, both circles have the same center *O*. The radii of the circles are 3 and 5.

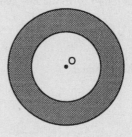

a Find, in terms of π, the area of the shaded region. [4]

b What percent of the diagram is unshaded? [2]

c A dart is thrown and lands on the diagram. Find the probability that the dart will land on the

(1) shaded area [2]
(2) unshaded area [2]

☞ GO RIGHT ON TO THE NEXT PAGE.

39 Solve algebraically for the positive value of x, $x \neq 0$, and check:

$$\frac{2x + 5}{7} = \frac{1}{x} \qquad [8,2]$$

40 The ages of three children in a family can be expressed as consecutive integers. The square of the age of the youngest child is 4 more than 8 times the age of the oldest child. Find the ages of the three children.   [10]

41 Solve the following system of equations algebraically or graphically and check:

$$3y = 2x - 6$$
$$x + y = 8 \qquad [8,2]$$

42 In $\triangle ABC$, AB is $\frac{3}{5}$ of the length of $\overline{BC}$, and AC is $\frac{4}{5}$ of the length of $\overline{BC}$. If the perimeter of $\triangle ABC$ is 24, find the lengths of $\overline{AB}$, $\overline{AC}$, and $\overline{BC}$. [*Only an algebraic solution will be accepted.*] [5,5]

Practice Test 2

Answers

1. $\sim p \rightarrow \sim q$

   Negate each of the statements.

2. 35

   It is the value that occurs most often.

3. $x = 5$

   To find the perimeter add the lengths of the sides.

   $x + x + 1 + 9 + 2x + 5 = 35$

   $4x + 15 = 35$ Subtract 15 from both sides.

   $4x = 20$

   $x = 5$

4. 70°

   m∠DGB + m∠BGF + m∠CGF = 180°   Straight line.

   $35 + \text{m}\angle BGF + 75 = 180$

   $\text{m}\angle BGF + 110 = 180$

   $\text{m}\angle BGF = 70$

   ∠AGE and ∠BGF are vertical angles and have the same measure, so $m\angle AGE = 70$.

5. 10

   Ratio of sides between the triangles is the same.

   $\dfrac{6}{24} = \dfrac{x}{40}$ Cross multiply.

   $240 = 24x$ Divide by 24.

   $10 = x$

6. $x = 13$

   The two angles are alternate interior angles and since the lines are parallel, the angles are equal.

   $4x + 30 = 7x - 9$ Subtract $4x$ from both sides.

   $4x + 30 - 4x = 7x - 9 - 4x$

   $30 = 3x - 9$ Add 9 to both sides.

   $39 = 3x$ Divide by 3.

   $13 = x$

7. $x = 11$

   $0.4x - 3 = 1.4$ Add 3 to both sides.

   $0.4x = 4.4$ Divide by .4.

   $x = 11$

8. $x = 22$

   $3x + 4 = 5(x - 8)$ Distribute 5.

   $3x + 4 = 5x - 40$ Subtract $3x$ from both sides.

   $4 = 2x - 40$ Add 40 to both sides.

   $44 = 2x$ Divide by 2.

   $22 = x$

9. $2x^2 + 11x - 21$

   Distribute.

   $2x(x + 7) - 3(x + 7)$

   $2x^2 + 14x - 3x - 21$

   $2x^2 + 11x - 21$

10. $p \rightarrow q$

    Negate each statement remembering that the negation of a negation of a statement is that statement.

11. 24

    The base of the parallelogram is 6 and the height is 4 so the area is $6 \times 4 = 24$ units sq.

12. 3

    If the equation is solved for y the coefficient of x is the slope.

13. 24

    We multiplied the x value by 3 so the y value should also be multiplied by 3.

14. 15

    Let h = hypotenuse, then use the Pythagorean Theorem.
    $h^2 = 9^2 + 12^2 = 81 + 144$
    $h^2 = 225$
    $h = 15$

15. $(x - 8)(x + 3)$

    $x^2 - 5x - 24$ Need factors of -24 that add up to -5. The factors are -8 and 3.

16. (2) $p \wedge \sim q$

    And is represented by $\wedge$.

17. (4)

    Using the multiplication principle. Since there are 5 shirts and 7 ties, there are 5×7 different choices.

18. (2)

    There are 4 marbles that are not green out of a total of 9 marbles, so the probability is $\frac{4}{9}$.

19. (4)

    An octagon has 8 sides, if it is regular all sides have the same length. The perimeter is the sum of the lengths of all 8 sides, $8(2x - 1)$ or $16x - 8$.

20. (3)

    Multiply.
    $$\frac{2a^3}{5b} \cdot \frac{3a^2}{7b} = \frac{6a^5}{35b^2}$$

21. (2)

    The additive inverse of $-4a$ is the expression that when added to $-4a$ will result in 0.

22. (4)

    The numbers between -4 and 2, including -4 but not 2.

23. (4)
    $$3\sqrt{5} + 6\sqrt{5} = 9\sqrt{5}$$

24. (3)

    3 makes the denominator equal to 0.

25. (1)

    Supplementary angles add to $180°$.

26. (3)

    Rewrite and cancel common factors.
    $$\frac{5!}{3!} = \frac{5 \cdot 4 \cdot 3 \cdot 2 \cdot 1}{3 \cdot 2 \cdot 1} = 20$$

27. (3)

    Substitute
    $2((.6)(5))^3 = 2(3)^3 = 2(27) = 54$

28. (1)

    Add together and divide by 2
    $4y + 3 + 2y - 1 = 6y + 2 = 2(3y + 1)$
    Dividing by 2 yields $3y + 1$.

29. (2)

    The letter A has only vertical line symmetry,
    the letter H has both vertical and horizontal
    line symmetry, and the letter F has no line
    of symmetry.

30. (1)

$x + ay = b$	Subtract x from both sides.
$ay = b - x$	Divide both sides by a.
$y = \dfrac{b - x}{a}$	

31. (3)

    $$\frac{28x^3 - 36x^2 = 4x}{4x} = \frac{28x^3}{4x} - \frac{36x^2}{4x} + \frac{4x}{4x} =$$
    $7x^2 - 9x + 1$

32. (2)

Area $= \pi(\text{radius})^2$	so
$100\pi = \pi r^2$	Divide by π.
$100 = r^2$	
$r = 10$	

33. (1)

    Rewrite with common denominator of 20.
    $$\frac{4y}{5} + \frac{3y}{4} = \frac{16y}{20} + \frac{15y}{20} = \frac{31y}{20}$$

34. (3)

$2x^2 + 5x - 3 = 0$	Factor.
$(2x - 1)(x + 3) = 0$	Set each factor equal to zero.

$2x - 1 = 0$	$x + 3 = 0$
$2x = 1$	$x = -3$
$x = \dfrac{1}{2}$	

35. (4)

    The shape did not change size, it was just
    translated.

36. a. 17

    Three intervals are less than 23 minutes and
    $2 + 6 + 9 = 17$.

    b. $23-25$
       There are 36 observations and the
       median is between the 18th and 19th
       observation which is in the $23-25$
       interval.

    c.

Interval	Cum. Freq.	
$14-16$	2	
$14-19$	8	$2 + 6$
$14-22$	17	$2 + 6 + 9$
$14-25$	25	$2 + 6 + 9 + 8$
$14-28$	32	$2 + 6 + 9 + 8 + 7$
$14-31$	36	$2 + 6 + 9 + 8 + 7$

d.

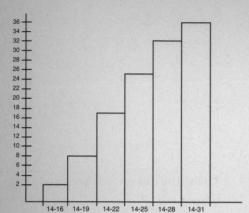

37. a. $\sim q \to \sim p$

Interchange the if—then parts.

b. If the food is not cooking, then the water is not boiling.

c. The stove is hot or the food is not cooking.

d.

p	q	$\sim q$	$p \wedge \sim q$
T	T	F	F
T	F	T	T
F	T	F	F
F	F	T	F

38. a. 16π

Area of big circle $= \pi(5)^2 = 25\pi$

Area of small circle $= \pi(3)^2 = 9\pi$

Shaded area $= 25\pi - 9\pi = 16\pi$

b. 36 percent

Unshaded area $= 9\pi$

$$\frac{9\pi}{25\pi} = \frac{9}{25} = \frac{36}{100}$$

c. (1) $\dfrac{16}{25}$

Shaded area $= 16\pi$, and the probability is

$$\frac{16\pi}{25\pi} = \frac{16}{25}$$

d. (2) $\dfrac{9}{25}$

Unshaded area $= 9\pi$, and the probability is

$$\frac{9\pi}{25\pi} = \frac{9}{25}$$

39. $x = 1$

$\dfrac{2x + 5}{7} = \dfrac{1}{x}$ — Cross multiply.

$x(2x + 5) = 7$

$2x^2 + 5x = 7$ — Subtract 7 from both sides.

$2x^2 + 5x - 7 = 0$ — Factor.

$(2x + 7)(x - 1) = 0$ — Set each factor equal to 0.

$2x + 7 = 0$ $x - 1 = 0$

$x = -\dfrac{7}{2}$ $x = 1$

Check $x = 1$

$\dfrac{2(1) + 5}{7} = \dfrac{1}{1}$

$\dfrac{2 + 5}{7} = 1$

$\dfrac{7}{7} = 1$

$1 = 1$

40. 10, 11, 12

    Let x = age of youngest child, then

    $x + 1$ = age of middle child, and

    $x + 2$ = age of oldest child.

    $x^2 = 4 + 8(x + 2)$

    $x^2 = 4 + 8x + 16$

    $x^2 = 8x + 20$ Subtract $8x$ and 20 from both sides.

    $x^2 - 8x - 20 = 0$ Factor.

    $(x - 10)(x + 2) = 0$ Set each factor equal to 0.

    $x - 10 = 0$ $x + 2 = 0$

    $x = 10$ $x = -2$

    Children are 10, 11, and 12.

41. (6, 2)

    Solve $x + y = 8$ for x, getting $x = 8 - y$.

    Then substitute into $3y = 2x - 6$ getting

    $3y = 2(8 - y) - 6$.

    $3y = 16 - 2y - 6$

    $3y = 10 - 2y$ Add $2y$ to both sides.

    $5y = 10$ Divide by 5.

    $y = 2$

    Substitute $y = 2$ into $x = 8 - y$ to get

    $x = 8 - 2 = 6$

    Check (6, 2).

    $3(2) = 2(6) - 6$ $6 + 2 = 8$

    $6 = 12 - 6$ Checks.

    Checks.

Graphically, we have this:

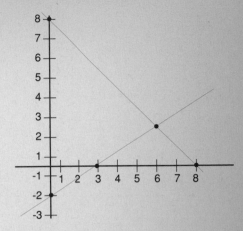

Checking this would be the same as with the algebraic solution.

42. $BC = 10$, $AB = 6$, and $AC = 8$

    Let x = length of $\overline{BC}$, then

    $\frac{3}{5}x$ = length of $\overline{AB}$, and

    $\frac{4}{5}x$ = length of $\overline{AC}$.

    $x + \frac{3}{5}x + \frac{4}{5}x = 24$

    $x + \frac{7}{5}x = 24$ Multiply both sides by 5.

    $5x + 5 \cdot \frac{7}{5}x = 24 \cdot 5$

    $5x + 7x = 120$

    $12x = 120$

    $x = 10$

    So the length of $\overline{AB}$ is $\frac{3}{5} \cdot 10 = \frac{30}{5} = 6$ and

    the length of $\overline{AC}$ is $\frac{4}{5} \cdot 10 = \frac{40}{5} = 8$.

Practice Test 3

Answer 30 questions from this part. Each correct answer will receive 2 credits. No partial credit will be allowed. Write your answers in the spaces provided on the separate answer sheet. Where applicable, answers may be left in terms of π or in radical form.   [60]

1 If 3 times a number is decreased by 5, the result is 7. Find the number.

2 Let p represent "Mr. Sanchez teaches mathematics" and let q represent "Mr. Sanchez coaches the soccer team." Using p and q, write in symbolic form: "If Mr. Sanchez teaches mathematics, then he does not coach the soccer team."

3 Express 7.8×10^3 as an integer.

4 What is the probability that a digit chosen at random from the set {1,2,3,4,5,6,7,8} will be a number divisible by 3?

5 Let p represent "I am well prepared" and let q represent "I will succeed." Using p and q, write in symbolic form: "I am well prepared and I will succeed."

6 In the accompanying diagram, lines $\overleftrightarrow{AB}$ and $\overleftrightarrow{CD}$ intersect at point E. If m$\angle CEB = 3x - 14$ and m$\angle AED = 31$, find the value of x.

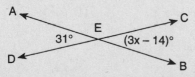

7 The volume of a rectangular solid is 24 cubic centimeters. If the width is 2 centimeters and the length is 3 centimeters, what is the height, in centimeters, of the solid?

8 In the accompanying figure, $ABCD$ is a square, $AB = 5x - 10$, and $BC = 2x + 20$. Find the value of x.

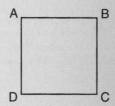

9 A school building has 8 entry doors on the first floor and 3 stairways to the second floor. In how many different ways can a person enter the building and go to the second floor?

10 A tree casts a shadow 30 feet long at the same time that a boy 5 feet tall casts a shadow 3 feet long. Find the height, in feet, of the tree.

11 In the accompanying diagram, parallel lines $\overleftrightarrow{AB}$ and $\overleftrightarrow{CD}$ intersect transversal $\overleftrightarrow{GH}$ at points E and F, respectively. If m$\angle AEG = 4x - 15$ and m$\angle CFE = 2x + 7$, find the value of x.

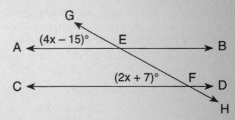

12 If $-18x^4y$ is divided by $-2xy$, what is the quotient?

13 Three numbers are represented by $2x$, $3x$, and $4x$. Find the value of x if the mean of the three numbers is 15.

14 Solve for x: $4(x + 3) = 2x - 8$

15 Solve the following system of equations for x:
$$2x + y = 10$$
$$3x - y = 15$$

16 Write in symbolic form the inverse of $s \rightarrow {\sim}t$.

17 In the accompanying diagram, the measure of exterior angle CBD is 110°. If the measures of the two nonadjacent interior angles are represented by $3x°$ and $2x°$, find the value of x.

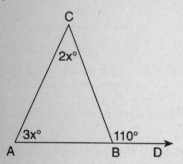

18 Find the sum of $4a^2 - 7a - 5$ and $-8a^2 - 2a + 7$.

19 Solve the equation $2x^2 - 98 = 0$ for the positive value of x.

Directions (20–35): For *each* question chosen, write on the separate answer sheet the *numeral* preceding the word or expression that best completes the statement or answers the question.

20 Which inequality is the solution of $x + 78 \geq 14$?
(1) $x \geq 92$ (3) $x \geq -64$
(2) $x \geq 64$ (4) $x \leq -92$

21 If $cx - d = f$, then x is equal to
(1) $f + d - c$ (3) $d + f$
(2) $\dfrac{f - d}{c}$ (4) $\dfrac{f + d}{c}$

22 Which diagram represents a reflection in line ℓ?

(1)
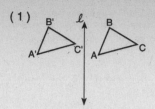

(2)
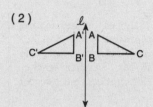

(3)
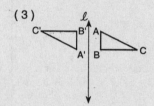

(4)
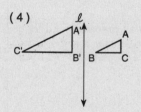

23 Which equation represents a line whose slope is $\frac{1}{2}$ and whose y-intercept is 3?
(1) $y = \frac{1}{2}x - 3$ (3) $y = 3x + \frac{1}{2}$
(2) $y = -\frac{1}{2}x + 3$ (4) $y = \frac{1}{2}x + 3$

24 The value of $\frac{6!}{2!}$ is
(1) 360   (3) 24
(2) 180   (4) 6

25 If y is an integer, what is the solution set of $-3 \leq y < 2$?
(1) $\{-3,-2,-1,0,1\}$ (3) $\{-3,-2,-1\}$
(2) $\{-2,-1,0,1,2\}$ (4) $\{0,1\}$

26 Tickets for a music concert were purchased at the rate of 500 tickets in 20 minutes. At this rate, how many tickets were purchased in m minutes?

(1) $\frac{1}{25}m$ (3) $50m$

(2) $25m$ (4) $500m$

27 A 3-inch × 5-inch photograph is enlarged so that each side is doubled. What is the number of square inches in the area of the enlarged photograph?

(1) 15   (3) 30
(2) 16   (4) 60

28 When $x = 2$ and $y = 0.5$, which expression has the largest value?

(1) $x - y$ (3) $x \div y$
(2) $x + y$ (4) $x \cdot y$

29 Which shape has the greatest number of lines of symmetry?

(1) parallelogram   (3) rhombus
(2) rectangle   (4) square

30 What is the multiplicative inverse of $\frac{x}{2}$?

(1) 1   (3) $-\frac{x}{2}$

(2) $\frac{2}{x}$ (4) $2x$

31 Expressed as a single fraction, $\frac{5a}{2} - \frac{a}{3}$ is equivalent to

(1) $\frac{5}{6}$ (3) $\frac{13a}{6}$

(2) $\frac{4a}{6}$ (4) $2a$

32 In which graph does line ℓ have a negative slope?

(1) 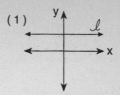   (3)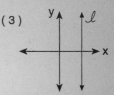

(2) 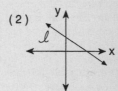   (4)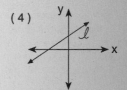

33 What is $5\sqrt{2} - \sqrt{18}$ expressed in simplest radical form?

(1) $2\sqrt{2}$ (3) $8\sqrt{2}$

(2) $-2\sqrt{2}$ (4) $-8\sqrt{2}$

34 If the lengths of the legs of a right triangle are 12 and 16, the length of the hypotenuse is

(1) 20   (3) 400
(2) 28   (4) $\sqrt{28}$

35 If two supplementary angles are in the ratio 4:5, the measure of the larger angle is

(1) 20°   (3) 100°
(2) 80°   (4) 120°

Answers to the following questions are to be written on paper provided by the school.

Part II

Answer four questions from this part. Clearly indicate the necessary steps, including appropriate formula substitutions, diagrams, graphs, charts, etc. Calculations that may be obtained by mental arithmetic or the calculator do not need to be shown. [40]

36 If the length of one side of a square is tripled and the length of an adjacent side is increased by 10, the resulting rectangle has an area that is 6 times the area of the original square. Find the length of a side of the original square. [10]

37 Construct and complete the truth table for the statement $(p \to q) \leftrightarrow \sim(p \wedge \sim q)$. [10]

38 *a* For all values of x for which these expressions are defined, perform the indicated operation and express in simplest form.

(1) $\dfrac{x + 2}{3} + \dfrac{x}{6}$ [3]

(2) $\dfrac{x + 2}{3} \cdot \dfrac{9}{x}$ [3]

b The distance an object falls is given by the formula $d = \frac{1}{2}gt^2$. Find d, to the *nearest tenth*, when $g = 9.8$ and $t = 4\frac{1}{2}$. [4]

39 On a Course I test, the scores of ten students were 90, 83, 82, 95, 96, 67, 88, 91, 82, and 86.

a Find the
(1) mean [1]
(2) median [2]
(3) mode [1]

b Find the probability that the score of a student chosen at random will be
(1) less than the mean [2]
(2) greater than the median [2]
(3) greater than or equal to the mode [2]

40 *a* Solve the following system of equations graphically:

$$y = 2x$$
$$x + y = 6$$ [6]

b Solve the system of equations given in part *a* algebraically. [4]

41 Rectangle *ABCD* is inscribed in circle *O* with the center on diagonal $\overline{BD}$ of the rectangle. The length of $\overline{BD}$ is 10 and the length of $\overline{BC}$ is 5.

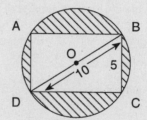

a Find, in simplest radical form, the
(1) length of $\overline{DC}$ [4]
(2) area of the rectangle [2]

b Find, to the *nearest integer*, the area of the shaded region. [4]

42 The larger of two negative numbers is five more than the smaller. If the square of the larger number is increased by 27, the result is the smaller number multiplied by −7. Find the numbers. [*Only an algebraic solution will be accepted.*] [5,5]

Practice Test 3

Answers

1. 4

   Let x = number

   $3x - 5 = 7$ Add 5 to both sides.

   $3x = 12$ Divide both sides by 3.

   $x = 4$

2. $p \rightarrow \sim q$

   not q is represented by $\sim q$

3. 7,800

   $7.8 \times 10^3 = 7.8 \times 1,000 = 7,800$

4. $\dfrac{2}{8}$

   3 and 6 are the only numbers divisible by three. Two numbers out of eight.

   The probability is $\dfrac{2}{8}$ or $\dfrac{1}{4}$.

5. $p \wedge q$

   $\wedge$ is the symbol for and.

6. 15

   $\angle CEB$ and $\angle AED$ are vertical angles so they have the same measure.

   $3x - 14 = 31$ Add 14 to both sides.

   $3x = 45$ Divide both sides by 3.

   $x = 15$

7. 4 cm

   $V = l \cdot w \cdot h$, so

   $24 = 3 \cdot 2 \cdot h$

   $24 = 6h$ Divide both sides by 6.

   $4 = h$

8. 10

   The sides of a square have the same length, so

   $5x - 10 = 2x + 20$ Subtract $2x$ from both sides.

   $3x - 10 = 20$ Add 10 to both sides.

   $3x = 30$ Divide both sides by 3.

   $x = 10$

9. 24

   Using the multiplication principle, there are 8 doors on first floor and 3 stairways, so there are 8×3 ways to the second floor.

10. 50 ft.

    Set up ratios of actual height to shadow.

    $\dfrac{5}{3} = \dfrac{t}{30}$ Cross multiply.

    $150 = 3t$ Divide both sides by 3.

    $50 = t$

11. $x = 11$

$\angle AEG$ and $\angle CFE$ are corresponding angles and since the lines are parallel, the angles are equal.

$4x - 15 = 2x + 7$ Subtract $2x$ from both sides.

$2x - 15 = 7$ Add 15 to both sides.

$2x = 22$ Divide both sides by 2.

$x = 11$

12. $9x^3$

$$-\frac{18x^4y}{-2xy} = \left(\frac{-18}{-2}\right)\left(\frac{x^4}{x}\right)\left(\frac{y}{y}\right) = 9x^3$$

13. $x = 5$

$$\frac{2x + 3x + 4x}{3} = 15 \quad \text{Multiply both sides by 3.}$$

$2x + 3x + 4x = 45$

$9x = 45$ Divide both sides by 9.

$x = 5$

14. $x = -10$

$4(x + 3) = 2x - 8$ Distribute 4.

$4x + 12 = 2x - 8$ Subtract $2x$ from both sides.

$2x + 12 = -8$ Subtract 12 from both sides.

$2x = -20$ Divide by 2.

$x = -10$

15. $x = 5$

Add the two equations to eliminate y.

$2x + y = 10$
$3x - y = 15$

$5x = 25$ Divide by 5.

$x = 5$

16. $\sim s \rightarrow t$

Negate each statement.

17. $x = 22$

$2x + 3x = 110$

$5x = 110$ Divide by 5.

$x = 22$

18. $-4a^2 - 9a + 2$

$(4a^2 - 7a - 5) + (-8a^2 - 2a + 7)$

    Combine like terms.

$= 4a^2 - 7a - 5 - 8a^2 - 2a + 7$

$-4a^2 - 9a + 2$

19. $x = 7$

$2x^2 - 98 = 0$ Add 98 to both sides.

$2x^2 = 98$ Divide by 2.

$x^2 = 49$

$x = \pm 7$ There are two numbers which squared equal 49. They are 7 and -7.

20. (3)

$x + 78 \geq 14$ Subtract 78 from both sides.

$x \geq -64$

21. (4)

$cx - d = f$ Add d to both sides.
$cx = d + f$ Divide both sides
                      by c.

$$x = \frac{d+f}{c}$$

22. (2)

It reflects the image across ℓ. (3) changes direction, (4) changes size, and (1) is not reflected.

23. (4)

When the equation is solved for y the slope is the coefficient of x and the constant term is the $y-$intercept.

24. (1)

Rewrite and cancel common factors

$$\frac{6!}{2!} = \frac{6 \cdot 5 \cdot 4 \cdot 3 \cdot 2 \cdot 1}{2 \cdot 1} = 6 \cdot 5 \cdot 4 \cdot 3 = 360$$

25. (1)

Need integers between -3 and 2 and the integer -3, but not the integer 2.

26. (2)

The rate at which tickets are purchased is $\frac{500 \text{ tickets}}{20 \text{ minutes}}$, which is 25 tickets per minute.

In m minutes, $25 \frac{\text{tickets}}{\text{minutes}} \times m$ minutes, which is $25m$ tickets will be purchased.

27. (4)

Enlarge to a 6 inch $\times$ 10 inch whose area is $6 \times 10 = 60$ sq. inches.

28. (3)

$x - y = 2 - 0.5 = 1.5; x + y = 2 + 0.5 = 2.5$
$x \div y = 2 \div 0.5 = 4; \ x \cdot y = 2 \times 0.5 = 1$

29. (4)

A square has four lines of symmetry.

30. (2)

The multiplicative inverse is the same as the reciprocal.

31. (3)

$\frac{5a}{2} - \frac{a}{3}$ Rewrite with the common denominator of 6.

$$\frac{15a}{6} - \frac{2a}{6} = \frac{13a}{6}$$

32. (2)

Negative slope slants down from left to right.

33. (1)

$5\sqrt{2} - \sqrt{18} = 5\sqrt{2} - \sqrt{9}\sqrt{2} = 5\sqrt{2} - 3\sqrt{2} = 2\sqrt{2}$

34. (1)

Using the Pythagorean Theorem:
$h^2 = 12^2 + 16^2 = 144 + 256$
$h^2 = 400$
$h = 20$

35. (3)

If the ratio is 4:5 then the larger angle is $\dfrac{5}{9}$ of the total. If two angles are supplementary, their total is 180.

$$\dfrac{5}{\cancel{9}} \times \overset{20}{\cancel{180}} = 100$$

36. $s = 10$

Let s = side of square, then
$3s$ and $s + 10$ are dimensions of new rectangle
Area of rectangle = $3s(s + 10)$, Area of square = s^2
$3s(s + 10) = 6s^2$

$3s^2 + 30s = 6s^2$	Get one side equal to zero.
$0 = 3s^2 - 30s$	Factor.
$0 = 3s(s - 10)$	Set each factor equal to zero.

$s = 0$ $s - 10 = 0$
$s = 10$

37.

p	q	$p \rightarrow q$	$\sim q$	$p \wedge \sim q$	$\sim(p \wedge \sim q)$	$(p \rightarrow q) \leftrightarrow \sim(p \wedge \sim q)$
T	T	T	F	F	T	T
T	F	F	T	T	F	T
F	T	T	F	F	T	T
F	F	T	F	T	T	T

38. a. (1) $\dfrac{3x + 4}{6}$

The expression is defined for all x.

$\dfrac{x + 2}{3} + \dfrac{x}{6}$ Rewrite with the common denominator of 6.

$\dfrac{2(x + 2)}{6} + \dfrac{x}{6}$

$\dfrac{2x + 4}{6} + \dfrac{x}{6} = \dfrac{3x + 4}{6}$

(2) The expression defined for all $x \neq 0$.

$\dfrac{x + 2}{\cancel{3}} \cdot \dfrac{\overset{3}{\cancel{9}}}{x}$

Cancel common factor of 3 between numerator and denominator

$\dfrac{3(x + 2)}{x} = \dfrac{3x + 6}{x}$

b. 99.2

$d = \dfrac{1}{2}(9.8)\left(\dfrac{9}{2}\right)^2$

$= .5(9.8)(4.5)^2$

$= .5(9.8)(20.25)$

$= 99.225$

$= 99.2$ to nearest tenth.

39. a.   (1) 86

$$\frac{90 + 83 + 82 + 95 + 96 + 67 + 88 + 91 + 82 + 86}{10}$$

$$= \frac{860}{10} = 86$$

   (2) 87

   Arrange scores in order from smallest to largest.

   67, 82, 82, 83, 86, 88, 90, 91, 95, 96.

   There are an even number of scores, 10, so the median will be the average of the two middle terms, 86 and 88, which is 87.

   (3) 82

   The mode is the score that occurs most often, in this case 82.

   b.   (1) $\frac{2}{5}$

   There are 4 scores out of 10 less than the mean.

   $$\frac{4}{10} = \frac{2}{5}$$

   (2) $\frac{1}{2}$

   There are 5 scores out of 10 greater than the median.

   $$\frac{5}{10} = \frac{1}{2}$$

   (3) $\frac{9}{10}$

   There are nine scores out of 10 greater than or equal to 82.

40. a. (2, 4)

   To graph an equation find two points.

   To graph $y = 2x$, let $x = 0$; then $y = 0$ and $(0, 0)$ is a point on the line.

   Let $x = 1$, then $y = 2$ and $(1, 2)$ is a point on the line.

   To graph $x + y = 6$

   Let $x = 0$, then $y = 6$ and $(0, 6)$ is a point on the line.

   Let $y = 0$, then $x = 6$ and $(6, 0)$ is a point on the line.

   Graph and find point of intersection.

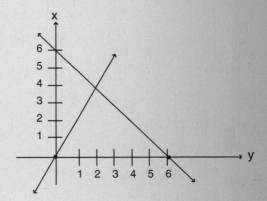

   The lines intersect at the point (2, 4).

   b. (2, 4).

   Use $y = 2x$ and substitute into $x + y = 6$ to get

   $x + 2x = 6$

   $3x = 6$ Divide by 3.

   $x = 2$

   Substitute in $y = 2x$ to get $y = 2(2) = 4$

41. a. (1)

Let x = length of $\overline{DC}$ and use the Pythagorean Theorem.

$10^2 = 5^2 + x^2$

$100 = 25 + x^2$

$75 = x^2$

$\sqrt{75} = \sqrt{x^2}$

$x = \sqrt{75} = \sqrt{25} \cdot \sqrt{3} = 5\sqrt{3}$

(2) $25\sqrt{3}$

Area = length $\times$ width = $5\sqrt{3} \times 5 = 25\sqrt{3}$

b.   35

Area of circle = $\pi(\text{radius})^2 = \pi(5)^2 = 25\pi$

Shaded area = $25\pi - 25\sqrt{3}$

$= 25(3.14) - 25(1.73)$

$= 78.5 - 43.25$

$= 35.25$

Nearest integer is 35.

42. $-13, -8$

Let x = smaller negative number, then $x + 5$ = larger negative number.

$(x + 5)^2 + 27 = -7x$

$x^2 + 10x + 25 + 27 = -7x$

$x^2 + 10x + 52 = -7x$ Add $7x$ to both sides.

$x^2 + 17x + 52 = 0$ Factor.

$(x + 13)(x + 4) = 0$ Set each factor equal to zero.

$x + 13 = 0$ $x + 4 = 0$

$x = -13$ $x = -4 \rightarrow$ Not both negative.

$x + 5 = -8$ $x + 5 = 1$

Practice Test 4

Part I

Answer 30 questions from this part. Each correct answer will receive 2 credits. No partial credit will be allowed. Write your answers in the spaces provided on the separate answer sheet. Where applicable, answers may be left in terms of π or in radical form. [60]

1 If the probability of snow tomorrow is $\frac{2}{5}$, what is the probability of no snow tomorrow?

2 Let p represent "Today is Monday" and let q represent "I am tired." Using p and q, write in symbolic form: "Today is Monday and I am not tired."

3 If a letter is chosen at random from the ten letters in the word "SEQUENTIAL," find the probability that the letter chosen is an "E."

4 In six computer games, Olga scored 122, 138, 130, 98, 102, and 124. What was the mean of her scores?

5 Solve for x: $1.4x - 0.9 = 3.3$

6 Let p represent "The triangle is equilateral," and let q represent "The triangle is a right triangle." Using p and q, write in symbolic form: "If the triangle is a right triangle, then it is not equilateral."

7 If 25% of a number is 12, find the number.

8 Solve for x: $\frac{7}{10}x + 2 = 16$

9 In the accompanying diagram, $\overleftrightarrow{AB}$ and $\overleftrightarrow{CD}$ intersect at E. If m$\angle AED = 2x + 11$ and m$\angle CEB = 5x - 19$, find the value of x.

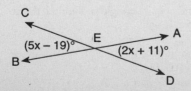

10 The area of a circle is 25π. What is the length of a radius of the circle?

11 A girl 5 feet tall casts a shadow of 2 feet. At the same time, a nearby tree casts a shadow of 24 feet. Find the number of feet in the height of the tree.

12 If x varies directly as y and $x = 8$ when $y = 4$, find x when $y = 16$.

13 Find the value of $5xy^2$ if $x = -2$ and $y = -3$.

14 In the accompanying diagram, parallel lines $\overleftrightarrow{AB}$ and $\overleftrightarrow{CD}$ are intersected by transversal $\overleftrightarrow{EF}$ at G and H, respectively. If m$\angle CHG = x + 20$ and m$\angle DHG = 3x$, find the value of x.

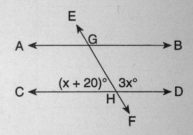

15 Expressed in radical form, what is the product of $2\sqrt{7}$ and $3\sqrt{5}$?

16 The larger angle of two supplementary angles has a measure of 20° more than the measure of the smaller angle. Find the number of degrees in the measure of the *smaller* angle.

175

17 In the accompanying diagram, m∠A = x + 20, m∠B = 3x, ∠BCD is an exterior angle formed by extending $\overline{AC}$ to point D, and m∠BCD = 120. Find the value of x.

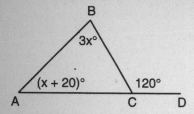

18 Solve for x: $9x - 4(x - 3) = 72$

19 Solve the following system of equations for y:
$$2x + y = 12$$
$$-2x + 3y = -4$$

20 What is the additive inverse of $-\dfrac{a}{2}$?

21 The test scores for 20 students in a Spanish class are shown in the frequency table below. In which interval does the upper quartile lie?

Interval	Frequency
90–99	4
80–89	6
70–79	5
60–69	4
50–59	1

Directions (22–35): For *each* question chosen, write on the separate answer sheet the *numeral* preceding the word or expression that best completes the statement or answers the question.

22 What is the quotient of $\dfrac{26x^4y^2}{13xy}$, $x \neq 0$, $y \neq 0$?

(1) $2x^4y^2$ (3) $2x^3y$
(2) $13x^5y^3$ (4) $13x^3y$

23 The two acute angles in an isosceles right triangle must measure
(1) 30° and 60°   (3) 40° and 50°
(2) 35° and 55°   (4) 45° and 45°

24 What is the value of $_5P_1$?
(1) 1   (3) 24
(2) 5   (4) 120

25 The perimeter of a square is 20x − 4. Which expression represents a side of the square in terms of x?
(1) 5x   (3) 8x − 16
(2) 10x − 2   (4) 5x − 1

26 Which number is *not* a member of the solution set of the inequality 4x ≥ 18?
(1) 4.4   (3) 4.6
(2) 4.5   (4) 4.7

27 What is the sum of $\dfrac{x - 1}{3}$ and $\dfrac{x + 3}{5}$?

(1) $\dfrac{x + 1}{4}$ (3) $\dfrac{8x + 4}{15}$

(2) $\dfrac{8x + 2}{15}$ (4) $\dfrac{x^2 + 2x - 3}{15}$

28 Which figure can *not* have both pairs of opposite sides parallel?
(1) parallelogram   (3) rhombus
(2) rectangle   (4) trapezoid

29 Which is a rational number?
(1) $\sqrt{7}$ (3) $\sqrt{49}$
(2) $\sqrt{18}$ (4) $\sqrt{20}$

30 If each side of a rectangle is doubled, the area of the rectangle will
(1) double
(2) be multiplied by 4
(3) be divided by 2
(4) remain the same

31 The accompanying diagram shows a right triangle.

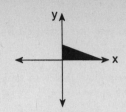

If the triangle is rotated 90° counterclockwise about the origin, what will the image be?

(1)

(3)

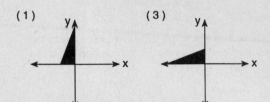

(2)

(4)

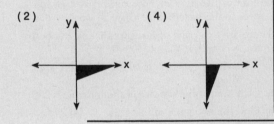

32 Which statement is true about the graph of the line whose equation is $y = 8$?

(1) The line is parallel to the x-axis.
(2) The line is parallel to the y-axis.
(3) The line passes through the origin.
(4) The line has a slope of 8.

33 The solution set of $x^2 - 5x + 6 = 0$ is

(1) {1,5}   (3) {2,3}
(2) {−1,−5}   (4) {−2,−3}

34 The length of the hypotenuse of a right triangle is 20 centimeters and the length of one leg is 12 centimeters. The length of the other leg is

(1) 8 cm   (3) 32 cm

(2) 16 cm   (4) $\sqrt{544}$ cm

35 Which sentence illustrates the associative property for multiplication?

(1) $ab = ba$
(2) $a(bc) = (ab)c$
(3) $a \cdot 1 = a$
(4) $a(b + c) = ab + ac$

Answers to the following questions are to be written on paper provided by the school.

Part II

Answer four questions from this part. Clearly indicate the necessary steps, including appropriate formula substitutions, diagrams, graphs, charts, etc. Calculations that may be obtained by mental arithmetic or the calculator do not need to be shown.   [40]

36 James is four years younger than Austin. If three times James' age is increased by the square of Austin's age, the result is 28. Find the ages of James and Austin. [*Only an algebraic solution will be accepted.*]   [4,6]

37 Write an equation or a system of equations that can be used to solve *each* of the following problems. In *each* case, state what the variable or variables represent. [*Solution of the equations is not required.*]

a The sum of two numbers is 240. The larger number is 6 less than twice the smaller. Find the numbers.   [5]

b In the accompanying diagram of isosceles trapezoid *ABCD*, *AB* = *CD*. The measure of ∠*B* is 40° more than the measure of ∠*A*. Find m∠*A* and m∠*B*.   [5]

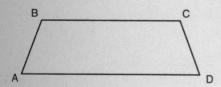

38 A jar contains four balls. Each ball has one letter printed on it. The letters are *A*, *E*, *D*, and *G*. One ball is drawn from the jar and its letter is noted. A second ball is then drawn without replacing the first and its letter is noted.

a Draw a tree diagram or list the sample space showing all possible outcomes.   [4]

b Find the probability that the letters printed on the two balls drawn consist of

(1) *at least* one vowel   [2]
(2) no vowels   [2]
(3) the same letter   [2]

39 Construct and complete the truth table for the statement ~$(q \land \neg p) \leftrightarrow (p \lor q)$.   [10]

40 *a* On the same set of coordinate axes, graph the following system of inequalities:

$$y \leq -4x + 6$$
$$y > \tfrac{2}{5}x - 5$$ [8]

b Based on the graph drawn in part *a*, write the coordinates of a point in the solution set of this system.   [2]

41 Use any method — algebraic, trial and error, making a table, etc. — to solve this problem. A written explanation of how you arrived at your answer is also acceptable. Show all work.

There are two pairs of integers that satisfy both of these conditions:

The smaller integer is 10 less than the larger integer.
The sum of the squares of the integers is 250.

a Find the two pairs of integers.   [8]

b Show that one pair of integers found in part *a* satisfies both given conditions.   [2]

42 Pentagon *RSTUV* has coordinates *R*(1,4), *S*(5,0), *T*(3,−4), *U*(−1,−4), and *V*(−3,0).

a *On graph paper*, plot pentagon *RSTUV*.   [2]

b Draw the line of symmetry of pentagon *RSTUV* and label the line *b*.   [2]

c Find the area of

(1) triangle *RVS*   [2]
(2) trapezoid *STUV*   [3]
(3) pentagon *RSTUV*   [1]

Practice Test 4

Answers

1. $\frac{3}{5}$

    The total probability is 1, so $1 - \frac{2}{5} = \frac{3}{5}$ is the probability of no snow.

2. $p \wedge \sim q$

    $\wedge$ is the symbol for *and*, also $\sim q$ represents *not q*.

3. $\frac{1}{5}$

    There are 2 E's among 10 letters and $\frac{2}{10} = \frac{1}{5}$.

4. 119

    $$\frac{122 + 138 + 130 + 98 + 102 + 124}{6} =$$

    $$\frac{714}{6} = 119$$

5. 3

    $1.4x - 0.9 = 3.3$ Add 0.9 to both sides.
    $1.4x = 4.2$ Divide by 1.4.
    $x = 3$

6. $q \rightarrow \sim p$

    To negate a statement use $\sim$.

7. 48

    Use ratios. 25 is $\frac{25}{100}$.

    $\frac{25}{100} = \frac{12}{x}$ Cross multiply.

    $25x = 1200$ Divide by 25.

    $x = 48$

8. $x = 20$

    $\frac{7}{10}x + 2 = 16$ Multiply both sides by 10.

    $10 \cdot \frac{7}{10}x + 10 \cdot 2 = 16 \cdot 10$

    $7x + 20 = 160$ Subtract 20 from both sides.

    $7x = 140$ Divide both sides by 7.

    $x = 20$

9. $x = 10$

    $\angle AED$ and $\angle CEB$ are vertical angles and have the same measure.

    $5x - 19 = 2x + 11$ Subtract $2x$ from both sides.

    $3x - 19 = 11$ Add 19 to both sides.

    $3x = 30$ Divide both sides by 3.

    $x = 10$

10. 5

    Area $= \pi(\text{radius})^2$
    $25\pi = \pi r^2$ Divide by π.
    $25 = r^2$
    $5 = r$

11. 60

    Using ratios

    $\frac{5}{2} = \frac{t}{24}$ Cross multiply.

$2t = 120$

$t = 60$

12. 32

Since x is double y and $y = 16$, $x = 32$.

13. -90

$5xy^2 = 5(-2)(-3)^2 = (-10)(9) = -90$

14. $x = 40$

$\angle CHG$ and $\angle DHG$ form a straight line, so they are supplementary.

$x + 20 + 3x = 180$

$4x + 20 = 180$ Subtract 20 from both sides.

$4x = 160$ Divide by 4.

$x = 40$

15. $6\sqrt{35}$

$2\sqrt{7} \times 3\sqrt{5} = (2 \times 3) \times (\sqrt{7} \times \sqrt{5}) = 6\sqrt{35}$

16. 80

Let x = measure of smaller angle, then

$x + 20$ = measure of larger angle

$x + x + 20 = 180$

$2x + 20 = 180$ Subtract 20 from both sides.

$2x = 160$ Divide by 2.

$x = 80$

17. $x = 25$

$3x + x + 20 = 120$

$4x + 20 = 120$ Subtract 20 from both sides.

$4x = 100$ Divide by 4.

$x = 25$

18. $x = 12$

$9x - 4(x - 3) = 72$ Distribute.

$9x - 4x + 12 = 72$

$5x + 12 = 72$ Subtract 12 from both sides.

$5x = 60$

$x = 12$

19. $y = 2$

Add the equations together.

$2x + y = 12$

$\underline{-2x + 3y = -4}$

$4y = 8$ Divide by 4.

$y = 2$

20. $\dfrac{a}{2}$

An additive inverse has the opposite sign.

21. 80–89

The upper quartile is between the 15th and 16th piece of data from the smallest to largest, which is in the interval $80-89$.

22. (3)

$\dfrac{26x^4y^2}{13xy} = \left(\dfrac{26}{13}\right)\left(\dfrac{x^4}{x}\right)\left(\dfrac{y^2}{y}\right) =$

$2x^{4-1}y^{2-1} = 2x^3y$

23. (4)

The angles must have the same measure and add up to 90.

24. (2)

$_5P_1 = \dfrac{5!}{4!} = \dfrac{5 \cdot 4 \cdot 3 \cdot 2 \cdot 1}{4 \cdot 3 \cdot 2 \cdot 1} = 5$

25. (4)

The perimeter is 4 times the length of a side. Since $20x - 4 = 4(5x - 1)$, the length of a side is $5x - 1$.

26. (1)

$4x \geq 18$ Divide by 4.

$x \geq 4.5$

27. (3)

$\dfrac{x-1}{3} + \dfrac{x+3}{5}$ Rewrite with a common denominator of 15.

$\dfrac{5(x-1)}{15} + \dfrac{3(x+3)}{15}$

$\dfrac{5x-5}{15} + \dfrac{3x+9}{15}$

$\dfrac{8x+4}{15}$

28. (4)

A trapezoid has only one pair of parallel sides.

29. (3)

Because $\sqrt{49} = 7$.

30. (2)

Each dimension is doubled, then multiplied together, which is equivalent to the product of the original length and width being multiplied by four.

31. (1)

It will rotate one quadrant to the left.

32. (1)

The graph is a horizontal line.

33. (3)

$x^2 - 5x + 6 = 0$ Factor.

$(x - 3)(x - 2) = 0$ Set each factor equal to zero.

$x - 3 = 0$ $x - 2 = 0$

$x = 3$ $x = 2$

34. (2)

Let ℓ = length of leg. Using the Pythagorean Theorem:

$20^2 = 12^2 + \ell^2$

$400 = 144 + \ell^2$

$256 = \ell^2$

$\sqrt{256} = \sqrt{\ell^2}$

$16 = \ell$

35. (2)

The associative property states that for any real numbers, a, b, and c, $a(bc) = (ab)c$. That is, when multiplying three numbers written in a specific order, the first number multiplied by the product of the second and third numbers is equal to the product of the first two numbers multiplied by the third number.

36. Austin is 5 and James is 1.

Let x = Austin's age, then

$x - 4$ = James's age.

$3(x - 4) + x^2 = 28$

$3x - 12 + x^2 = 28$ Get the right side equal to zero by subtracting 28 from both sides.

$x^2 + 3x - 40 = 0$ Factor.

$(x + 8)(x - 5) = 0$ Set each factor equal to zero.

$x + 8 = 0$ $x - 5 = 0$

$x = -8$ (not possible) $x = 5$

$x - 4 = 1$

37. a. $x + 2x - 6 = 240$

Let x = smaller number, then

$2x - 6$ = larger number.

$x + 2x - 6 = 240$

b. $x + x + 40 = 180$

Let $x = m\angle A$, then $x + 40 = m\angle B$

Since $\overline{AD} \| \overline{BC}$, $m\angle A + m\angle B = 180°$, so $x + x + 40 = 180$.

38. a.

First ball   A   E   D   G

         /|\   /|\   /|\   /|\

        E D G   A D G   A E G   A E D

Sample space {AE, AD, AG, EA, ED, EG, DA, DE, DG, GA, GE, GD}

b.   (1) $\dfrac{5}{6}$

10 possibilities out of 12 have at least one vowel, and $\dfrac{10}{12} = \dfrac{5}{6}$.

(2) $\dfrac{1}{6}$

2 possibilities out of 12 have no vowels and $\dfrac{2}{12} = \dfrac{1}{6}$.

(3) 0

No outcome has the same letter.

39.

p	q	$\sim p$	$q \wedge \sim p$	$\sim(q \wedge \sim p)$	$p \vee q$	$\sim(q \wedge \sim p) \leftrightarrow (p \vee q)$
T	T	F	F	T	T	T
T	F	F	F	T	T	T
F	T	T	T	F	T	F
F	F	T	F	T	F	F

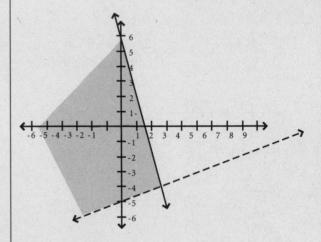

40. To graph $y \le -4x + 6$

Let $x = 0$, $y = 6$. Let $y = 0$, $x = {}^3\!/_2$. Need a solid line.

Check $(0, 0)$ $0 \le -4(0) + 6$. True— shade below the solid line.

To graph $y > \dfrac{2}{5}x - 5$

Let $x = 0$, $y = -5$. Let $x = 5$, $y = -3$. Need a solid line.

Check $(0, 0)$ $0 > \dfrac{2}{5}(0) - 5$ True. Shade above the dotted line.

Final graph has shaded the overlap of the above.

b. $(1, -1)$ other answers are possible.
Any point in above shaded region.

41. a.

15, 5 and $-15, -5$

Let x = larger integer, then

$x - 10$ = smaller integer.

$x^2 + (x - 10)^2 = 250$

$x^2 + x^2 - 20x + 100 = 250$

$2x^2 - 20x + 100 = 250$ Subtract 250 from both sides.

$2x^2 - 20x - 150 = 0$ Divide by 2.

$x^2 - 10x - 75 = 0$ Factor.

$(x-15)(x+5) = 0$ Set each factor equal to zero.

$x - 15 = 0$ $x + 5 = 0$

$x = 15$ $x = -5$

$x - 10 = 5$ $x - 10 = -15$

b. $5 = 15 - 10$

$5^2 + 15^2 = 25 + 225 = 250$

42. a. and b.

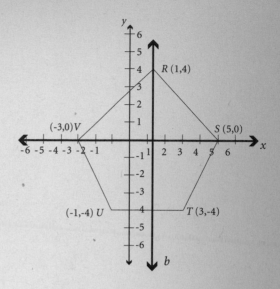

c. (1) 16

The base of the triangle is 8, the height is 4. The area is $\frac{1}{2} \cdot 8 \cdot 4 = 16$.

(2) 24

The bases of the trapezoid are 8 and 4, the height is 4. The area is

$$\frac{1}{2} \cdot (8 + 4) \cdot 4 = 2(12) = 24$$

(3) 40

The pentagon is made up of the above two regions, so the area is $16 + 24 = 40$.

Practice Test 5

Part I

Answer 30 questions from this part. Each correct answer will receive 2 credits. No partial credit will be allowed. Write your answers in the spaces provided on the separate answer sheet. Where applicable, answers may be left in terms of π or in radical form.   [60]

1 The sections of a spinner are shaded in blue and yellow. The probability that the spinner will land on a blue section is $\frac{4}{9}$. What is the probability that the spinner will *not* land on a blue section?

2 The Earth is approximately 93,000,000 miles from the Sun. If this distance is expressed as 9.3×10^n, what is the value of n?

3 Solve for x: $0.5x + 3 = 4.5$

4 If the scores 18, 20, 25, 11, and x have a mean of 19, what is the value of x?

5 In the accompanying diagram, $\overleftrightarrow{BC}$, $\overleftrightarrow{BAD}$, and $\overleftrightarrow{CAE}$ intersect to form $\triangle ABC$. If m$\angle ABC = 25$ and m$\angle C = 90$, find m$\angle DAE$.

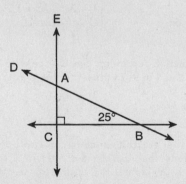

6 Factor: $y^2 - 100$

7 Two adjacent sides of a rhombus are represented by $5x + 7$ and $6x - 1$. Find the value of x.

8 If two angles are supplementary and one angle is twice as large as the other, find the number of degrees in the measure of the *smaller* angle.

9 Solve for x: $\frac{x}{7} - 5 = -4$

10 If y varies directly as x and $y = 24$ when $x = 4$, find the value of y when $x = 9$.

11 In the accompanying diagram of $\triangle ABC$, $\overline{AC}$ is extended to D, m$\angle BCD = 140$, and m$\angle ABC = 85$. Find m$\angle BAC$.

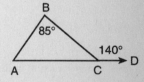

12 The sides of a triangle measure 9, 15, and 18. If the shortest side of a similar triangle measures 6, find the length of the longest side of this triangle.

13 In the accompanying diagram, K is the image of A after a translation. Under the same translation, which point is the image of J?

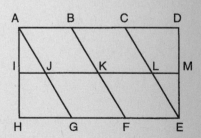

185

14 Write, in symbolic form, the inverse of $\sim e \rightarrow p$.

15 Point $(k,-2)$ lies on the line whose equation is $x - 3y = 7$. What is the value of k?

16 In the accompanying diagram, transversal $\overleftrightarrow{GH}$ intersects parallel lines $\overleftrightarrow{AB}$ and $\overleftrightarrow{CD}$, $m\angle DGH = x$, and $m\angle BHG = 2x - 30$. Find the value of x.

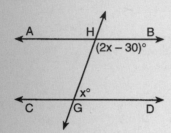

17 Solve for x in terms of a, b, and c:

$$ax - 3b = c$$

18 Express $\frac{3x}{4} - \frac{x}{5}$ as a single fraction in simplest form.

Directions (19–35): For *each* question chosen, write on the separate answer sheet the *numeral* preceding the word or expression that best completes the statement or answers the question.

19 If $n + 8$ represents an odd integer, the next larger odd integer is represented by
(1) $n + 10$ (3) $n + 7$
(2) $n + 9$ (4) $n + 6$

20 The product of $(-3xy^2)(5x^2y^3)$ is
(1) $-8x^3y^5$ (3) $-15x^2y^5$
(2) $-15x^3y^5$ (4) $-15x^3y^6$

21 What is the value of x in the equation $4(2x + 1) = 27 + 3(2x - 5)$?
(1) 21   (3) $7\frac{1}{2}$
(2) 9   (4) 4

22 Which letter has point symmetry?
(1) E   (3) H
(2) C   (4) T

23 The line whose equation is $y = 4x + 2$ has a y-intercept whose coordinates are
(1) (0,0)   (3) (4,0)
(2) (0,2)   (4) (0,4)

24 Which graph represents the inequality $-1 \leq x < 4$?

(1)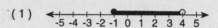

(2)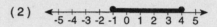

(3)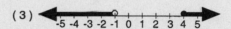

(4)

25 The expression $\dfrac{12z^4 + 20z^3 - 4z^2}{-4z^2}$, $z \neq 0$, is equivalent to
(1) $-4z^2$ (3) $-3z^2 - 5z + 1$
(2) $-3z^2 - 5z$ (4) $3z^2 - 5z - 1$

26 Which equation represents the line parallel to the y-axis and 4 units to the left of the y-axis?
(1) $x = 4$ (3) $y = -4$
(2) $x = -4$ (4) $y = 4$

27 What is the greatest number of two-letter arrangements that can be formed from the letters G, R, A, D, and E if each letter is used only once in an arrangement?
(1) 120   (3) 20
(2) 60   (4) 5

28 If two angles of a triangle each measure 70°, the triangle is described as
(1) right   (3) obtuse
(2) scalene   (4) isosceles

29 What is the value of the expression $2x^2 - 5x + 6$ when $x = -2$?

(1) 32   (3) 24
(2) -24   (4) 4

30 The value of $(7 - 2)!$ is

(1) 5   (3) 2520
(2) 120   (4) 5038

31 The expression $\sqrt{200}$ is equivalent to

(1) $2\sqrt{10}$ (3) $100\sqrt{2}$
(2) $10\sqrt{2}$ (4) $2\sqrt{100}$

32 Which statement has the same truth value as $\sim m \to p$?

(1) $m \to \sim p$ (3) $\sim p \to \sim m$
(2) $p \to \sim m$ (4) $\sim p \to m$

33 Which ordered pair is the solution set for this system of equations?

$$x + y = 8$$
$$y = x - 3$$

(1) (2.5,5.5)   (3) (4,4)
(2) (4,1)   (4) (5.5,2.5)

34 What is the solution set of the equation $x^2 - 7x - 18 = 0$?

(1) {9,-2}   (3) {-6,3}
(2) {-9,2}   (4) {6,-3}

35 When $a^2 + a - 3$ is subtracted from $3a^2 - 5$, the result is

(1) $2a^2 - a - 2$ (3) $-2a^2 + a + 2$
(2) $2a^2 - a + 2$ (4) $4a^2 + a - 8$

Answers to the following questions are to be written on paper provided by the school.

Part II

Answer four questions from this part. Clearly indicate the necessary steps, including appropriate formula substitutions, diagrams, graphs, charts, etc. Calculations that may be obtained by mental arithmetic or the calculator do not need to be shown.   [40]

36 *a* On the same set of axes, graph the following system of inequalities. Label the region that represents the solution set with an *S*.   [8]

$$y \geq 3x$$
$$x + y < 8$$

b Write the coordinates of a point that satisfies the inequality $y \geq 3x$ but does *not* satisfy the inequality $x + y < 8$.   [2]

37 Solve the following system of equations algebraically and check:

$$2x = 5y + 8$$
$$3x + 2y = 31$$ [8,2]

38 Find four consecutive positive integers such that the product of the first and fourth is four less than twice the first multiplied by the fourth. [*Only an algebraic solution will be accepted.*]   [4,6]

39 A restaurant sells large and small submarine sandwiches. Rolls for the sandwiches are ordered from a baker. The roll for a large sandwich costs $0.25 and the roll for a small sandwich costs $0.15. Melissa, the manager of the restaurant, ordered 130 more large rolls than small rolls. What was the greatest number of large rolls she received if she spent *less than* $63? [*Show or explain the procedure used to obtain your answer.*]   [10]

40 The frequency table below shows the scores on a science quiz.

Interval	Frequency
90–99	6
80–89	8
70–79	10
60–69	4
50–59	2

a Based on the frequency table, which interval contains the median?   [2]

b Which interval contains the 70th percentile?   [2]

c On your answer paper, copy and complete the cumulative frequency table below.   [2]

Interval	Cumulative Frequency
50–99	
50–89	
50–79	
50–69	
50–59	2

d On graph paper, using the cumulative frequency table completed in part *c*, construct a cumulative frequency histogram.   [4]

GO RIGHT ON TO THE NEXT PAGE. ⟹

41 In the accompanying diagram, *ABCD* is an isosceles trapezoid with bases $\overline{AB}$ and $\overline{CD}$, $\overline{BA}$ is extended to *E*, and $\overline{DE} \perp \overline{EB}$. Side $\overline{BC}$ is a diameter of semicircle *O*, *AB* = 4, *AE* = 3, *DE* = 4, and *DC* = 10.

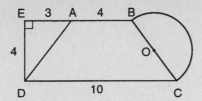

a Find the length of $\overline{AD}$.   [2]

b Find the area of the entire figure to the *nearest integer*.   [8]

42 Let *p* represent "It is raining" and let *q* represent "I am going swimming."

a Write *each* of these sentences in symbolic form.

   (1) It is not true that if it is raining, then I am going swimming.   [1]

   (2) It is raining and I am not going swimming.   [1]

b Construct a truth table for the two sentences written in part *a* to determine whether or not the sentences are logically equivalent. Justify your answer.   [8]

Practice Test 5

Answers

1. $\dfrac{5}{9}$

    $1 - \dfrac{4}{9} = \dfrac{5}{9}$

2. 7

    $93{,}000{,}000 = 9.3 \times 10^7$ since the decimal point must be moved 7 places.

3. 3

    $0.5x + 3 = 4.5$

    $0.5x = 1.5$

    $x = 3$

4. 21

    $\dfrac{18 + 20 + 25 + 11 + x}{5} = 19$

    $74 + x = 95$

    $x = 21$

5. 65

    $m\angle CAB + 90 + 25 = 180$ since all are angles of $\triangle CAB$.

    $m\angle CAB + 115 = 180$

    $m\angle CAB = 65$. Angles $\angle CAB$ and $\angle DAE$ are vertical angles and thus have the same measure.

6. $(y - 10)(y + 10)$

    Difference of the two squares.

7. 8

    All sides of a rhombus have the same length.

    $5x + 7 = 6x - 1$

    $x = 8$

8. 60

    Let $x =$ the smaller angle, then $2x =$ the larger angle. Supplementary means their sum is 180.

    $x + 2x = 180$

    $3x = 180$

    $x = 60$

9. 7

    $\dfrac{x}{7} - 5 = -4$

    Multiply by 7.

    $x - 35 = -28$

    $x = 7$

10. 54

    If $y = 24$ when $x = 4$, then $y = 6x$.

    If $x = 9$, then $y = 54$.

11. 55

    $m\angle A + m\angle B = m\angle BCD$

    $m\angle A + 85 = 140$

    $m\angle A = 55$

12. 12

$$\frac{6}{9} = \frac{\ell}{18} \qquad \text{Cross multiply.}$$

$$108 = 9\ell$$

$$12 = \ell$$

13. F

A traveled over to the right one letter and down one letter.

14. $e \rightarrow \sim p$

Negate both statements.

15. 1

Plug in -2 for y and solve for x.

$$x - 3(-2) = 7$$

$$x + 6 = 7$$

$$x = 1$$

16. 70

$$x + 2x - 30 = 180$$

$$3x - 30 = 180$$

$$3x = 210, \ x = 70$$

17. $\dfrac{c + 3b}{a}$

$$ax - 3b = c$$

$$ax = c + 3b$$

$$x = \frac{c + 3b}{a}$$

18. $\dfrac{11x}{20}$

$$\frac{3x}{4} - \frac{x}{5} \qquad \text{LCD is 20.}$$

$$\frac{15x}{20} - \frac{4x}{20} = \frac{11x}{20}$$

19. (1)

Odd integers are 2 apart:

$$n + 8 + 2 = n + 10.$$

20. (2)

$$(-3xy^2)(5x^2y^3) = (-3)(5)x1 + 2y^2 + 3 =$$

$$-15x^3y^5$$

21. (4)

$$4(2x + 1) = 27 + 3(2x - 5)$$

$$8x + 4 = 27 + 6x - 15$$

$$8x + 4 = 12 + 6x$$

$$2x = 8$$

$$x = 4$$

22. (3)

H has the point of symmetry which is the midpoint of its horizontal line segment.

23. (2)

The x value of the y intercept is always 0.

$$y = 4(0) + 2 = 2$$

24. (1)

Include the numbers between 1 and 4, include 1, but do not include 4.

25. (3)

$$\frac{12z^4}{-4z^2} + \frac{20z^3}{-4z^2} - \frac{4z^2}{-4z^2} = 3z^2 - 5z + 1$$

26. (2)

Lines parallel to y-axis are $x =$ number.

27. (3)

There are 5 choices for the first letter, and for each of these choices there are 4 choices for the second letter.

$5 \times 4 = 20$

28. (4)

If two angles have the same measure, then two sides have the same measure and the triangle is isosceles.

29. (3)

$2(-2)^2 - 5(-2) + 6 = 2(4) + 10 + 6 =$

$8 + 10 + 6 = 24$

30. (2)

$(7 - 2)! = 5! = 5 \times 3 \times 4 \times 2 \times 1 = 120$

31. (2)

$\sqrt{200} = \sqrt{100 \cdot 2} = \sqrt{100} \cdot \sqrt{2} \cdot = 10\sqrt{2}$

32. (4)

Negate the statements and change direction of implication.

33. (4)

Substitute $y = x - 3$ into $x + y = 8$

$x + x - 3 = 8; 2x - 3 = 8; 2x = 11; x = 5.5$

$y = 5.5 - 3 = 2.5$

34. (1)

$x^2 - 7x - 18 = 0$

$(x - 9)(x + 2) = 0$ Set each factor equal to zero.

$x - 9 = 0 \quad x + 2 = 0$

$x = 9 \qquad x = -2$

35. (1)

$3a^2 - 5 - (a^2 + a - 3) =$

$3a^2 - 5 - a^2 - a + 3 =$

$2a^2 - a - 2$

36. a.

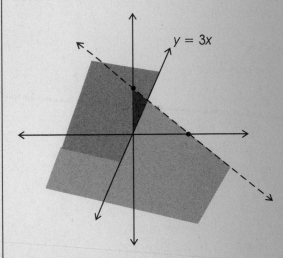

$y \geq 3x \qquad x + y < 8$

x	y		x	y
0	0		0	8
1	3		8	0
2	6		4	4

Test (1, 1)   Test (0, 0)

$1 + 1 \geq 3$ NO $0 + 0 < 8$ YES

Shade other side.   Shade that side.

b. (0, 9)

There are a lot of possible answers.

37. $(9, 2)$

$2x - 5y = 8$
Eliminate x by multiplying both sides of the first equation, $2x - 5y = 8$, by 3 and multiplying both sides of the second equation, $3x - 2y = 31$, by -2.

$6x - 15y = 24$
$-6x - 4y = -62$
_____

$-19y = -38$
$y = 2$

$2x - 5(2) = 8$
$2x - 10 = 8$
$2x = 18 \quad x = 9$

38. $1, 2, 3, 4$

Let x = first, $x + 1$ = second, $x + 2$ = third, and $x + 3$ = fourth.

$x(x + 3) = 2x(x + 3) - 4$
$x^2 + 3x = 2x^2 + 6x - 4$
$0 = x^2 + 3x - 4$
$0 = (x + 4)(x - 1)$

$x + 4 = 0 \qquad\qquad x - 1 = 0$
$x = -4 \qquad\qquad x = 1$
$x + 1 = 2$
$x + 2 = 3$
$x + 3 = 4$

39. 206

Let x = number of large rolls.
$x - 130$ = number of small rolls.

$.25x + .15(x - 130) < 63$ Multiply both sides by 100.

$25x + 15(x - 130) < 6300$
$25x + 15x - 1950 < 6300$
$40x < 8250$
$x < 206.25$

40. a. $70 - 79$

There are 30 scores, the median is between the 15th and 16th in the 70–79 range.

b. $80 - 89$

There are 30 scores. Let the scores be arranged in order from smallest to largest. Now $.7(30) = 21$. The 21st score is in the 80-89 interval.

c.

Interval	Cum. Freq.
50–99	30
50–89	24
50–79	16
50–69	6
50–59	2

d.

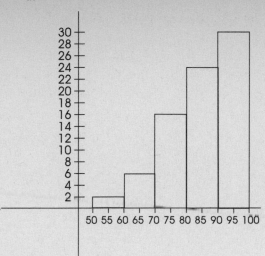

41.a. 5

Pythagorean Theorem

$3^2 + 4^2 = AD^2$

$9 + 16 = AD^2$

$25 = AD^2$

$5 = AD$

b. 44

The figure is made up of a triangle, trapezoid, and semicircle.

Area of triangle $= \frac{1}{2}(4)(3) = 6$

Area of trapezoid $= \frac{1}{2}(4)(4 + 10) = 2(14)$
$= 28$

Area of semicircle $=$

$\frac{1}{2}\pi\left(\frac{5}{2}\right)^2 = \frac{1}{2} \cdot \pi \cdot \frac{25}{4} = \frac{25\pi}{8}$

$6 + 28 + \frac{25\pi}{8} \approx 34 + 9.8 = 43.8 \approx 44$

42. a. (1) $\sim (p \rightarrow q)$

To represent it is not true, use $\sim$.

To represent "If it is raining, then I am going swimming," use $p \rightarrow q$.

(2) $p \wedge \sim q$

Use p to represent raining, use $\wedge$ to represent "and," and use $\sim q$ to represent not going swimming.

b.

p	q	$p \rightarrow q$	$\sim(p \rightarrow q)$	$\sim q$	$p \wedge \sim q$
T	T	T	F	F	F
F	T	T	F	F	F
T	F	F	T	T	T
F	F	T	F	T	F

$\sim(p \rightarrow q)$ and $p \wedge \sim q$ are logically equivalent because they have the same truth value for each possible choice of truth values for p and q.

Subject Index

Notes

Notes

Notes

Notes

Notes

Notes

Notes

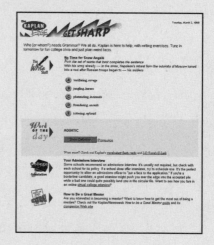

How Did We Do? Grade Us.

Thank you for choosing a Kaplan book. Your comments and suggestions are very useful to us. Please answer the following questions to assist us in our continued development of high-quality resources to meet your needs.

The Kaplan book I read was: _____

My name is: _____

My address is: _____

_____

My e-mail address is: _____

What overall grade would you give this book?   Ⓐ Ⓑ Ⓒ Ⓓ Ⓕ

How relevant was the information to your goals?   Ⓐ Ⓑ Ⓒ Ⓓ Ⓕ

How comprehensive was the information in this book?   Ⓐ Ⓑ Ⓒ Ⓓ Ⓕ

How accurate was the information in this book?   Ⓐ Ⓑ Ⓒ Ⓓ Ⓕ

How easy was the book to use?   Ⓐ Ⓑ Ⓒ Ⓓ Ⓕ

How appealing was the book's design?   Ⓐ Ⓑ Ⓒ Ⓓ Ⓕ

What were the book's strong points? _____

How could this book be improved? _____

Is there anything that we left out that you wanted to know more about?

Would you recommend this book to others?   ☐ YES   ☐ NO

Other comments: _____

_____

_____

Do we have permission to quote you?   ☐ YES   ☐ NO

Thank you for your help. Please tear out this page and mail it to:

Dave Chipps, Managing Editor
Kaplan Educational Centers
888 Seventh Avenue
New York, NY 10106

Or, you can answer these questions online at www.kaplan.com/talkback.

Thanks!

SIXTY · YEARS · OF
KAPLAN
60
BUILDING · FUTURES

Want more information about our services, products or the nearest Kaplan center?

1 **Call our nationwide toll-free numbers:**

1-800-KAP-TEST for information on our courses, private tutoring and admissions consulting
1-800-KAP-ITEM for information on our books and software
1-888-KAP-LOAN* for information on student loans

2 **Connect with us in cyberspace:**

On AOL, keyword: kaplan
On the World Wide Web, go to: www.kaplan.com
Via e-mail: info@kaplan.com

3 **Write to:**

Kaplan Educational Centers
888 Seventh Avenue
New York, NY 10106

About

Educational Centers

Kaplan Educational Centers is one of the nation's leading providers of premier education and career services. Kaplan is a wholly owned subsidiary of The Washington Post Company.

TEST PREPARATION & ADMISSIONS

Kaplan's nationally recognized test prep courses cover more than 20 standardized tests, including secondary school, college and graduate school entrance exams and foreign language and professional licensing exams. In addition, Kaplan offers private tutoring and comprehensive, one-to-one admissions and application advice for students applying to graduate programs. Kaplan also provides information and guidance on the financial aid process.

SCORE! EDUCATIONAL CENTERS

SCORE! after-school learning centers help K-8 students build confidence, academic and goal-setting skills in a motivating, sports-oriented environment. Its cutting-edge, interactive curriculum continually assesses and adapts to each child's academic needs and learning style. Enthusiastic Academic Coaches serve as positive role models, creating a high-energy atmosphere where learning is exciting and fun. SCORE! Prep provides in-home, one-on-one tutoring for high school academic subjects and standardized tests.

KAPLAN LEARNING SERVICES

Kaplan Learning Services provides customized assessment, education and professional development programs to K-12 schools and universities.

KAPLAN INTERNATIONAL PROGRAMS

Kaplan services international students and professionals in the U.S. through a series of intensive English language and test preparation programs. These programs are offered at Kaplan City Centers and four new campus-based centers in California, Washington and New York via Kaplan/LCP International Institute. Kaplan and Kaplan/LCP offer specialized services to sponsors including placement at top American universities, fellowship management, academic monitoring and reporting, and financial administration.

KAPLAN PUBLISHING

Kaplan Publishing produces books, software and online services. Kaplan Books, a joint imprint with Simon & Schuster, publishes titles in test preparation, admissions, education, career development and life skills; Kaplan and Newsweek jointly publish guides on getting into college, finding the right career, and helping your child succeed in school. Through an alliance with Knowledge Adventure, Kaplan publishes educational software for the K-12 retail and school markets.

KAPLAN PROFESSIONAL

Kaplan Professional provides recruitment and training services for corporate clients and individuals seeking to advance their careers. Member units include Kaplan Professional Career Services, the largest career fair provider in North America; Perfect Access/CRN, which delivers software education and consultation for law firms and businesses; HireSystems, which provides web-based hiring solutions; and Kaplan Professional Call Center Services, a total provider of services for the call center industry.

DISTANCE LEARNING DIVISION

Kaplan's distance learning programs include Concord School of Law, the nation's first online law school; and National Institute of Paralegal Arts and Sciences, a leading provider of degrees and certificates in paralegal studies and legal nurse consulting.

COMMUNITY OUTREACH

Kaplan provides educational resources to thousands of financially disadvantaged students annually, working closely with educational institutions, not-for-profit groups, government agencies and other grass roots organizations on a variety of national and local support programs. Kaplan enriches local communities by employing high school, college and graduate students, creating valuable work experiences for vast numbers of young people each year.